ALL ABOUT
FURNITURE REPAIR
& REFINISHING

*Created and designed
by the editorial staff
of ORTHO BOOKS*

Project Editor
Karin Shakery

Writers
Herbert Dunne
and the Editors of
Ortho Books

Illustrator
David M Kidd

Photographer
Douglas Manchee

Ortho Books

Publisher
Robert J. Dolezal

Production Director
Ernie S. Tasaki

Managing Editors
Karin Shakery
Michael D. Smith
Sally W. Smith

System Manager
Leonard D. Grotta

National Sales Manager
Charles H. Aydelotte

Marketing Specialist
Susan B. Boyle

Operations Coordinator
Georgiann Wright

Office Assistant
Deborah Tibbetts

Senior Technical Analyst
J. A. Crozier, Jr.

Address all inquiries to
Ortho Books
Chevron Chemical Company
Consumer Products Division
Box 5047
San Ramon, CA 94583

Copyright © 1987
Chevron Chemical Company
All rights reserved under international and Pan-American copyright conventions.

2	3	4	5	6	7	8	9
	88	89	90	91	92		

ISBN 0-89721-086-7
Library of Congress Catalog Card
Number 86-072436

Chevron Chemical Company
6001 Bollinger Canyon Road, San Ramon, CA 94583

Acknowledgments

Copy Chief
Melinda Levine

Editorial Coordinator
Kate Rider

Copyeditor
Judith Dunham

Proofreader
Andrea Y. Connolly

Editorial Assistant
Leslie Tilley

Indexer
Elinor Lindheimer

Composition and Pagination
Linda M. Bouchard

Production Coordinator
Deborah Cowder, Studio 165

Color Separations by
Color Tech

Lithographed in USA by
Webcrafters, Inc.

Additional Photographers

Laurie Black: Pages 54, 69
Fred Lyon: Page 49
Stephen Marley: Pages 3, 76, 77, 93
Kit Morris: Page 78

Consultants

Firenze Furniture
San Francisco, Calif.

"Hoot" Judkins
San Francisco, Calif.

David Daniels
General Transformations
Berkeley, Calif.

Special Thanks

The Antique Center
San Francisco, Calif.

The Chelsea Shop
San Francisco, Calif.

Circa Atelier
San Francisco, Calif.

Furniture Restoration Center
San Francisco, Calif.

The Strip Shop
San Francisco, Calif.

Designers

Larry Boyce
San Francisco, Calif.
Page 83

Carlos Marchiori
San Francisco, Calif.
Pages 74–75, 79, 92, Back cover

Molly McGowan
Oakland, Calif.
Page 93

Barry Nelson
San Francisco, Calif.
Pages 90, 91

The Painted Finish
San Francisco, Calif.
Page 82

Tony Pisacane
San Francisco, Calif.
Page 78

Ilene Sanford
Ilene Sanford Interior Designs
San Francisco, Calif.
Page 77

Antonio Torrice
Just Between Friends
San Francisco, Calif.
Page 7

Front Cover
Repairing an ornately carved Victorian reproduction of a Jacobean chair is well worth the effort. A bar clamp spans from side to side, holding glued joints in place until they dry.

Page 1. Replacing carving is difficult and may require professional skills.

Page 3
Top. Gleam on the pine table is provided by both the patina of age and the refinished surface.
Below. Corner blocks strengthen the joints of the antique dining chair that is also seen on the cover.

Back Cover
Top Left. The tools needed for refinishing can be found in most home workshops.
Top Right. Chipped or buckled veneer is a common flaw that requires repair work before refinishing can begin.
Bottom Left. If the wood doesn't warrant a clear finish, there are many painted effects that will breathe new life into a piece of furniture.
Bottom Right. Tools needed for painted effects are ordinary paint brushes.

ALL ABOUT
FURNITURE REPAIR & REFINISHING

Getting Started 5
Is it Worth the Effort? 6
Identifying Wood 8
Cleaning Versus Stripping 10
Fasteners 11
Glues 12
Clamps 14
Joinery 16

Repairing 19
Loose Joints 21
Chair Problems 22
Wobbly Tables 24
Warped Tops 25
Faulty Doors 26
Difficulties with Casters 28
Problems with Drawers 29
Missing Parts 30
Broken Runners 31
Broken Edges and Corners 32
Interior Defects 34
Uneven Legs 35
Repairing Veneer 36

Surfacing 39
Repairing Surfaces 40
Stripping 44
Sanding 48
Wood Fillers 52
Sealing 53
Staining 55

Finishing 59
Choosing a Clear Finish 60
Varnish 61
Shellac 66
Lacquer 70
Oil Finishes 72
Wax 73

Special Effects 75
Fun Furniture 76
Antiquing 80
Distressing 81
Marbling 82
Stenciling 83
Gilding 84
Bleaching 86
Fuming 88
Decoupage 89
Graining 90
Trompe l'Oeil 92
Enamel 93

Index 95
Metric Chart 96

GETTING STARTED

Refinishing and repairing furniture is one of the most satisfying of the many crafts that can be practiced by the do-it-yourselfer.

There is much pleasure in creating a glowing, sound piece of furniture out of a dreary, battered castoff that had been collecting dust in the attic or basement. Knowing that the transformation was the result of your handiwork is reward enough but if the piece has sentimental value, the gratification is all the greater.

Restoring furniture is fun, and while you are enjoying the satisfaction of looking at a creation of your own patient efforts, you can reflect on the fact that a well-restored piece will usually be worth more than a similar new piece.

Repairing and refinishing pieces of furniture enable the do-it-yourselfer to gradually accumulate a sizable collection of fine older pieces.

IS IT WORTH THE EFFORT?

This book is designed according to the logical sequence of steps that should be followed when repairing and refinishing a piece of furniture. But you can jump in at just about any point.

If you intend to work just on the surface, go directly to the section covering the type of finish you intend to apply. But remember that the final finish will emphasize, rather than obscure, any flaws that lie beneath it. In other words the end result can be only as good as the preparatory work.

Do-it-yourself work can be highly enjoyable, but only if things go right. The best way to be sure that they do is to take your time and familiarize yourself thoroughly with each procedure before setting out to accomplish it. Whatever your present level of expertise, make sure that the time you spend refurbishing furniture will give you satisfaction and that your efforts result in attractive pieces that will give pleasure and serve you well for years to come.

The rewards

There is much pleasure in creating a sound, glowing piece of furniture out of a dreary, battered castoff that has been collecting dust in the attic or basement. Knowing that the transformation is the result of your own handiwork is reward enough but, if the piece has sentimental value, the gratification is all the greater.

It may take a little imagination to see beyond split and broken rails and finishes buried under layers of paint, varnish, oil, and dust, but beauty will emerge if you are willing to see the

project through to the final polishing.

Another good reason for putting dilapidated furniture into first-class condition is that the rewards can yield material gain as well as personal satisfaction. Unless you are dealing with antiques (see Restoring Versus Refinishing, below) a good refinishing job results in a piece with a better resale value than its new counterpart.

Although some new furniture is of excellent quality, the price of good wood is so high nowadays that a large proportion of contemporary furniture is fashioned, at least in part, from plywood, particleboard, and plastic laminate. Unless hopelessly damaged, virtually any piece of older furniture, especially if it has hand-carving, is worth saving.

Restoring versus refinishing

Legally any piece of furniture made before 1830 is an antique. Loosely speaking any piece over 100 years old is considered an antique, and any work on it should be done by a restoration expert.

If you suspect that the piece under consideration is a genuine antique, or old enough to be considered such, seek professional advice. Part of the value lies in the original finish; stripping and refinishing will almost certainly reduce the value. An old pine cupboard with the original paint finish is worth considerably more than a similar piece that has been refinished. This is true even if the paint is so badly worn and crazed that, to the uninformed, it looks messy.

Unfinished furniture

Perhaps the reason you bought this book is to get some ideas for finishing a piece that has never been finished.

Unfinished furniture is widely available, reasonably priced, and comes in a large variety of styles ranging from clean-lined modern pieces to period reproductions. If the

quality of the wood makes it inappropriate to use a clear finish, look at the stenciling, marbling, and enameling sections in the chapter on Special Effects.

Suitability

There are many places to find solid, attractive pieces whose only faults are that they have become run down. If your storage areas—or those of your friends or relatives—don't yield anything suitable, look in thrift shops and second-hand stores or try auctions and classified ads.

Just because a certain piece is available free or for a nominal price doesn't mean that it is worth putting in the considerable amount of effort necessary to make it usable. Exercise the same care when choosing pieces for repair and refinishing as you would when buying new furniture.

Even if the piece has potential, consider whether you really like the look of it. Does it go with your other furniture? Can you really use it? Are there seriously damaged parts that will have to be replaced, either by yourself or a professional? Major rebuilding projects should probably be left until you have a certain amount of experience.

Necessary tools

Most of the equipment needed for both repairing and refinishing furniture can be found in the average home toolbox.

There are some repairs where a table saw and a lathe will make the work much easier, but if you don't own these tools, you can have the necessary parts made for you.

Unless you plan to do a lot of refinishing work, going out and buying a complete set of specialized clamps is not necessary. Either make a clamping device or rent clamps as you need them.

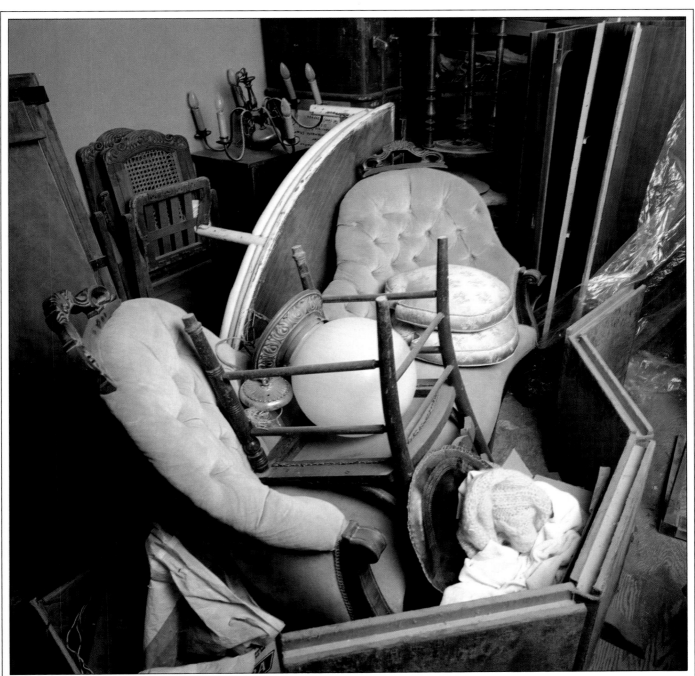

Flea markets, thrift shops, auction houses, and second-hand stores are some of the sources for furniture with potential. Many grubby-looking and undervalued older pieces can turn into gems when given tender loving care.

IDENTIFYING WOOD

It is important to know what species of wood has been used in the piece you intend to repair or refinish.

The choice of an appropriate finish depends to some extent on the type of wood. Is the wood hard or soft? Is it open- or close-grained? Old or new? Veneered or solid? All these considerations have some bearing on how the do-it-yourselfer should set to work. This is especially true when you work on pieces that have been refinished inappropriately, with a crudely painted or enameled surface.

Knowing the wood may give you a clue about what finish to choose—some are particularly attractive on certain kinds of wood. And when a piece needs a repair that calls for the addition of new wood, the do-it-yourselfer needs to know what wood to ask for when shopping.

Many pieces of furniture have areas of bare wood on the undersides, and sometimes the maker stamps this surface with the name of the wood used. If not, the wood can usually be identified quite easily by comparing color, grain, porosity, and other characteristics with that of wood samples or wood-sample photographs. Thin sheets of sample wood can also be obtained at many paint stores.

Bear in mind that the following short guide covers only the most widely used furniture woods. There are hundreds of other woods, including many exotic hardwoods that are sometimes used in furniture-making as inlays or veneers. If the wood you are trying to identify isn't on the list that follows, consult a professional. Remember also that different pieces of wood of the same species can appear different because of age, the mineral content of the soil where the tree grew, and the season of cutting.

Types of wood

Ash
A tough, heavy hardwood often used in chairs, particularly for bentwood pieces. Used for baseball bats and the wood of choice for tool handles. Usually grayish white but may have a rich brownish color. Marked grain patterns and open pores. Growth rings evident in end grain. Usually given a clear finish over bare or stained wood.

Beech
A dense, strong, and heavy hardwood. Pale cream colored, sometimes pink, flecked with brown. Often used for turned and bent work. Looks attractive with a clear finish over bare or stained wood. Often given a grained finish.

Birch
A strong, stiff, heavy hardwood, often used to imitate more expensive woods. Ranges in color from almost white to red-brown, but is usually cream colored. Fine texture and clear grain, either straight or in wavy rays, very small pores. Looks attractive with a clear finish over bare or stained wood. Frequently stained to simulate walnut or cherry.

Cedar
Fairly hard but brittle. Also known as aromatic red cedar because of the characteristic smell and color. Very pronounced knotty patterns. The aroma makes it a favorite as the raw material for storage chests. May be unfinished or given a clear finish.

Cherry
Quite hard with a tight grain that resists warping. Has a warm red-brown color that becomes richer as it ages, particularly with exposure to sunlight. Has small pores, doesn't require filling. Used for good-quality furniture. Looks best unstained with a clear finish.

Elm
English elm is a coarse-textured pale brown wood with an irregular grain. American elm, also called rock elm, is light brown and straight grained with light and dark striations. Fairly hard but bends well. Frequently used for bentwood chairs. Should be stained and given a clear finish.

Fir
Several firs are used in furniture manufacture; the most widely used is Douglas fir. Fir is a fairly hard wood often used for plywood. Often hidden by veneer. White to creamy yellow, sometimes light reddish brown. Very resinous with eccentric grain markings. May be given a clear finish over bare wood or stain. Must be sealed before being stained. Frequently painted with colored enamel.

Mahogany
Fairly hard and heavy, fine grained and durable. Three major types are available: tropical American, West Indian, and African. (Philippine mahoganies are not of the same species.) Typical color is deep red-brown. Used for solid or veneered furniture. Usually given a clear finish over bare wood, although older pieces were often stained.

Maple
Very hard and strong, with a fine, even texture. Also known as rock maple, sugar maple, and bird's-eye maple (because of the effect that sometimes appears in the grain). Usually straight grained with minute pores. White, cream-white, and amber. Used for furniture of the finest quality. Curly and bird's-eye patterns are used for high-grade veneers. Should be given a clear finish over bare or stained wood. Characteristic red of maple comes from staining.

Oak
Strong, hard, and durable. Turns and bends well; can be steamed. Has a marked grain that can be felt with the

fingers if not filled but can be given a high finish. May be filled or not depending on desired effect. Tannic acid in oak corrodes ferrous fittings. Ranges in color from light gray to pinkish brown. Often used for older furniture, still common on better modern pieces. Also used for figured veneers. Should be given a clear finish over stained or bare wood.

Pecan
This strong, durable wood is a member of the hickory family. Often used by cabinetmakers for Mediterranean- and Provincial-style furniture. Reddish-brown, often with dark streaks. May be finished in natural shades or stained to resemble walnut.

Pine
This soft wood is often used for unfinished pieces and for reproductions. Both eastern and western white pine are used for furniture and are very similar in appearance and characteristics: creamy white to ruddy brown with noticeable growth rings. May be clear finished over bare wood or stain. Should be sealed before staining and is often enameled.

Poplar
Quite light in weight and rather soft, with an even, fibrous texture. Also known as whitewood and tulipwood. Used for plywood and to simulate other woods. White, sometimes light yellow or yellowish brown. Should be stained and given a clear finish. Takes stain well and may be stained to resemble more expensive woods. Frequently painted with colored enamel.

Redwood
Strong and light but not very hard. Highly resistant to rot. Dark reddish brown with pronounced growth rings. Often used for lawn furniture because of weather-resistant properties. Almost always given a clear finish. Should not be stained.

Rosewood
Highly figured, extremely hard, and coarse textured. Dark purple or orange-brown with large pores. Aromatic, oily; takes a high finish. Often used for veneer on highest quality

furniture. Use only clear finishes. Should never be filled or stained.

Sycamore
Fairly hard, fine and even textured. Used for violins and tabletops. Distinctive growth pattern, small pores. Light brown, often with a reddish tinge. Clear finish over bare or stained wood.

Teak
Hard, slightly greasy, open grained, coarse, and tough. Tawny to dark brown with contrasting streaks. Fragrant; moisture and rot resistant. Used for modern furniture, sometimes as a veneer. Use a clear finish; penetrating oil is recommended.

Walnut
Strong, shock resistant, fine textured with close, highly figured grain. Sometimes known as black walnut. Bare wood is gray- or purple-brown; turns darker when given a clear finish. Takes a high finish. Can be bleached or stained yellow-orange or brown-red. Often given clear finish over bare wood.

CLEANING VERSUS STRIPPING

Techniques exist for dealing with most types of surface damage without removing the entire finish.

Use these reviving and patching methods whenever possible. If your efforts to rejuvenate an old finish fail, you won't have wasted much time. The methods for bringing new life to old finishes apply mainly to clear finishes such as varnish, shellac, lacquer, oil, and wax. Enameled furniture generally needs to be refinished because little can be done to repair badly damaged paint.

Cleaning
Often an old piece of furniture is so dirty that it looks as if it needs refinishing. However, a good washing may be all that is required to bring up the fine qualities of a finish that lies hidden under layers of grease, grime, smoke, and wax.

Using water
Water and wood are natural enemies, so restrict washing to pieces that have been enameled or varnished. Never wash a veneered piece of furniture—water dissolves the glue.

A thorough washing with warm water, detergent, and a little ammonia should determine whether the surface drabness is merely the result of years of accumulated dirt. Keep in mind that water whitens shellac and lacquer and that both finishes dissolve in ammonia. Be sure to test a small, inconspicuous area if you suspect that either of these finishes were used on your piece.

Using wood cleaners
Commercial wood cleaners are available in most home-center stores. These will remove stubborn grease spots and built-up dirt.

Look for a formulation that is based on mineral spirits. Avoid products that contain oil and claim to "condition" the wood. The object is to remove oily, waxy, greasy build-up, not to add to it. Also avoid heavy-duty cleaners such as TSP (trisodium phosphate) except in cases where the piece has been stored for years and is caked with dirt. Heavy-duty cleaners may damage the surface.

Determining the finish
Repair methods depend on both the nature of the damage and the kind of finish you are dealing with. These factors are usually interrelated. For example, a white haze on a tabletop is probably the effect of moisture on shellac or lacquer.

If wet drinking glasses have caused white rings, you can be sure that the piece has been shellacked or lacquered. Since both these finishes dissolve in solvent, it is often possible to respread them to produce a sparkling "new" finish. This process, known as reamalgamation (see page 40), only applies to finishes that consist of a resinous film that is left behind when the solvent has evaporated.

Enamels and paints are easy to identify by sight, but the clear finishes on older pieces may be varnish, shellac, or lacquer, and these can be difficult to distinguish from each other. Since commercially finished furniture is rarely varnished, the odds are that a clear finish is either lacquer or shellac. Pieces finished before 1920 are more likely to be shellacked, whereas those finished after that date are probably lacquered. There are several tests you can make.

Is it shellac?
Using a soft cloth or piece of cotton, apply denatured alcohol (shellac thinner) to an inconspicuous wax-free part of the finish. Rub briskly for several minutes. This treatment causes shellac to begin softening and spreading. Keep on rubbing; it may take a little while for the shellac to start dissolving.

Is it lacquer?
If the surface isn't shellac, lacquer thinner will determine whether it is lacquer or varnish. Lacquer always has a harder finish than varnish, but to be absolutely sure, rub on the thinner in one place for several minutes. Lacquer begins to soften and smear; varnish does not.

Is it varnish?
If the lacquer thinner causes the finish to crack and come loose in patches, the coating is varnish. To be absolutely sure, apply a little paint remover. If it is varnish. the surface will crinkle and soften.

It's possible to find treasures that have been discarded simply because they need some repair work and a good cleaning.

FASTENERS

S crews are the most usual fasteners for furniture work; nails are not generally used except to pin a joint or for authenticity.

Screws

As a general rule, screws should only be used for repair work when the repair is to a screw joint that has failed. Flat-head wood screws are the type normally used in furniture repair. Use these when the screw is to be countersunk (screwed down below the surface of the wood) and concealed with a wooden plug. Oval-head screws are used infrequently and only when the screw is meant to be visible. Use the original screws whenever possible when doing repairs or restoration. Replace damaged screws with new ones of the same size and type.

Sizes

The size numbers of screws give both the screw length and the diameter at the widest point. Screws used in

Conceal holes drilled for countersunk screws with wood filler or a wooden plug.

furniture are mostly ¾ inch to 1½ inches long, 8 to 16 gauge.

In general, the length of a screw should be about three times the thickness of the top piece being joined, although it is sometimes necessary to use a shorter screw to prevent it from penetrating through the lower piece.

Uses

Screws are typically used to join a surface section, such as a tabletop, to the frame of the piece. When used for this reason, screws are usually countersunk and concealed with wood plugs. Avoid driving screws into the end grain—they probably won't hold. When preparing to drill a screw hole, pencil an *X* at the point where a screw is to be driven. Place an awl at the center of the *X*. Lightly tap the awl with a hammer to mark the position and make a starting hole for the drill bit.

Joining hardwood. If you are joining two pieces of hardwood, the screw holes in the two pieces should be different sizes. The hole drilled in the upper piece (the pilot hole) should be large enough so that the screw can be put in with the fingers. For the screws to hold properly, the diameter of the lower hole (anchor hole) should be about one third less than that of the screw shank. Use a bit two sizes smaller than the shank diameter to give the necessary holding power. If using a flat-head screw, countersink the opening of the upper hole to take in the screw head so that it seats below or flush with the surface. Screws driven into hardwood go in more easily if rubbed with wax or soap.

Drill the pilot hole (smaller than the screw shank) first; then drill through the pilot hole to half its depth, to enlarge the hole for the unthreaded top half of the screw; finally countersink a recess to accommodate the screw head. Use a countersink bit to cut a recess for the screw head. (Drill bits that drill all three stages in one step are available.)

Joining softwood. Join two pieces of softwood with a screw that is driven

through two holes of the same diameter. Self-tapping screws, which do not require any sort of pilot hole, can be used successfully on softwoods.

It's important to use a screwdriver of the correct size. Ideally, the blade of the screwdriver should be exactly the width of the slot in the screw. If the size is off by more than just a bit, either the head will be damaged or the screw will be hard to fully tighten.

A convention exists among wood workers to align the slots in screw heads, which creates a more pleasing visual effect. On horizontal surfaces line up the slots with the grain of the wood; on vertical surfaces, the slots should be parallel to the floor.

Hard-to-remove screws can often be jarred loose with a hammer. Put the blade of the screwdriver in the screw slot and give the handle a sharp blow with a hammer, simultaneously turning the screwdriver in a counterclockwise direction.

Nails

The use of nails in furniture work is not encouraged. Where metal fasteners are required, screws almost always do a better job. If nails are used, drive them beneath the surface with a nail set and conceal them with stick shellac. Do not use nails to strengthen weak joints; more often than not, they have the opposite effect.

There are, however, a couple of legitimate uses of nails in furniture repair: to pin a dowel joint and to hold a drawer base in place. Instructions for these uses appear where these subjects are discussed.

Nails can be used for repair work in the interest of authenticity if the original fastenings were nails. Glued joints in many nineteenth-century pieces were reinforced with square nails. If possible use the original fasteners when making repairs to older pieces. Replicas of old nails are available from specialty shops, but if you can't locate suitable ones, make the repair with glued dowels.

GLUES

Choosing the right glue is half the job. Various glues are used in furniture work, but for most purposes, the choice narrows to only four: white glue, yellow glue, epoxy, and contact cement.

Types of glue

Whatever glue you choose, always read the manufacturer's instructions before starting to work. Minor details about suitability and application can make the difference between a successful bond and a failure.

White glue

Also known as PVA (polyvinyl acetate) glue, white glue is a popular and effective general adhesive for furniture. It comes ready to use and sets quickly. Use white or yellow glue where convenience is more important than a really strong bond.

Yellow glue

Yellow glue is an improved version of white glue. It bonds more strongly than white, fills gaps better, and dries more quickly. If a joint is not as perfectly fitted as it might be, yellow glue fills more and secures better than white glue.

White glue and yellow glue are the best glues for most jobs. The fact that neither is waterproof is not a significant disadvantage since wood itself is harmed by water. Neither glue should be used on outdoor furniture.

Epoxy

Epoxy is the strongest adhesive available. It comes in two parts, resin and hardener, which are mixed just before use. Epoxy can be used lavishly as a filler because it is the one type of glue that is stronger than the wood it bonds. And since epoxy can be sanded after it sets, gaps filled with it can be shaped to follow the line of the wood.

Although epoxy requires little or no clamping to form a solid bond (it sets rather than dries), many woodworkers do use clamps to be on the safe side. If it weren't expensive and messy and time-consuming to mix, epoxy would be the only glue ever needed for furniture repair. White and yellow glues work just as well, however, for most applications.

Epoxy is completely water-resistant—it will even set under water—so it is the glue of choice for lawn furniture and other outdoor pieces.

Contact cement

Contact cements are useful for bonding sheetlike materials such as veneers, plastic laminates, and leather. These cements set almost instantly, so take care in positioning the section to be adhered—it will stick as soon as it makes contact.

Animal and fish glues

These glues are still used by purists who restore antiques. Except for this sort of insistence on extreme authenticity, there is no good reason to use these obsolete materials.

Miscellaneous glues

Other glues that are used in furniture work are resorcinol, urethane, and various plastic resin substances, but none of these has a significant advantage over epoxy and white and yellow glues. Resorcinol is an excellent glue for outdoor furniture because it is completely water-resistant.

Applying glue

There are three secrets to good gluing: Apply glue sparingly ("less is more" is a good rule for gluing), clamp tightly, and allow plenty of time for drying. It is best to allow glue to dry for at least 24 hours before doing any further work on the piece. Temperature is also a factor—don't try to glue if either the glue or the wood is too cold. Temperatures below 70° F are unsuitable for gluing.

A properly glued joint is at least as strong as the wood itself, but a poorly glued joint is much weaker. Restrict repairs to joints that are actually loose; leave firm, tight joints in place. Disassemble them if it is the only way to gain access to other joints.

A useful tool for repairing loose joints is the glue injector. This is a relatively inexpensive plastic device that works on the principle of a hypodermic syringe and delivers glue into small cracks and fissures. However, seriously loosened joints must be taken apart and reglued.

If disassembly of a joint containing animal or fish glue is necessary, soaking it with warm vinegar will loosen the adhesive. But modern glues made of plastic resins will not respond to this treatment.

You may be able to simply pull loose joints apart. Those that can't be pulled apart can be knocked apart by gentle tapping with a hammer or a wooden or rubber mallet. Protect the furniture from direct blows by using a block of wood or a thick pad of folded newspaper. If a lot of hammering is needed, construct a special block faced with sheet cork to protect the wood.

Surfaces to be glued should be absolutely clean. All traces of dirt, wax, finish, and old glue must be removed before beginning.

Whether surfaces to be glued should be rough or smooth is debatable. Some experts believe that any surface that is to be glued should be roughened slightly, either by sanding or by scoring lightly with a knife; others insist that this is unnecessary and may even weaken the bond. Although roughening may add strength, modern glues bond so well that you get strong joints whether or not the wood is roughened.

Surfaces to be glued must fit together well. Check the fit after the parts are thoroughly cleaned by clamping them before applying glue. If they fit, disassemble the parts and apply a thin layer of glue to both surfaces. (Use slightly more glue on end grain—it is more absorbent.) Reassemble the pieces, clamp them, wipe away excess glue, and check for correct alignment.

Be sure to use clamps or tourniquets to apply pressure: The single most important step in gluing is clamping since drying joints must be held immobile. This ensures that the elements bond together properly. Use slivers of wood or folded newspaper to protect the wood surfaces from the contact points of the clamps or tourniquets. As soon as the clamps are tight, wipe off all excess glue from the finish.

When all gluing and clamping has been completed, test the piece for stability and alignment of parts. For obvious reasons, don't wait for the glue to dry before checking to see if the piece is true. Use a T-square or a carpenter's level to check for level surfaces and correct angles. Alignment should be checked in all possible directions. Spot-check alignment as the glue dries to make sure that the force of the clamps has not pulled the piece out of true. Allow the glue to dry overnight, at least; it's best to wait two days before doing any further work on the piece.

There will usually be some dried glue left around the joint after the clamps or tourniquets are removed. Glue that is outside the joint is absolutely useless as well as unsightly. Carefully scrape away all traces of dried glue using a knife blade.

Using white glue is an effective way to repair a loose rung, but be sure that surfaces to be glued are absolutely clean. For a strong joint all traces of dirt, wax, old finish, and old glue must be removed.

CLAMPS

C lamps are essential equipment for furniture work. Successful joint gluing depends on them.

Types of clamps

Several types of clamps are available, and each type is manufactured in many different sizes.

C-clamps

These are the most generally useful clamps for furniture work. The clamping surfaces are small metal pads that are adjusted by turning a screw handle. Therefore, it is always necessary to use folded newspaper or thin strips of soft wood to prevent the clamp from biting into the wood. (Pieces of cork sliced from a bottle stopper are ideal.) Clamps and tourniquets can be improvised from strong tape, clothespins, rubber bands, and pieces of rope.

Wood clamps

Also known as screw clamps and Jorgensen clamps, wood clamps are the traditional clamps for furniture work, although they are not as versatile as C-clamps. Because the clamping surfaces are hardwood, they don't mar the furniture. Wood clamps adjust easily, set at any angle, and come in many sizes, from miniatures to versions that open to 14 inches.

Bar clamps

Bar clamps and pipe clamps, which are similar, are necessary for holding wide pieces of wood. They consist of two movable jaws fitted over a metal bar or pipe, which is available in lengths from 1 to 4 feet. Use these to hold cabinet sides, tabletops, and chair seats. They are usually used in pairs, so two is the minimum for most home workshops; you may need four for gluing large pieces. Bar clamps are rather expensive, so if you don't expect to have much use for them after the project at hand is complete, rent them for a few days.

As with C-clamps, always use folded newspaper or thin strips of wood as padding between the clamp and the surface of the furniture.

Tourniquets

Tourniquets, also known as strap clamps, can be used in place of wood clamps and bar clamps. A tourniquet consists of a fabric strap fitted with a bucklelike metal clamp. The strap is pulled tight around the pieces and clamped in place; it is further tightened by turning a nut on the clamp.

Tourniquets are inexpensive, but they can also be improvised using a piece of rope and a short stick or dowel. Loop a piece of rope around the pieces to be joined, then loop it again. Tighten the rope and tie the ends. Insert a stick between the two loops and twist to the desired tension. Lodge the stick behind a heavy object to keep the tension constant.

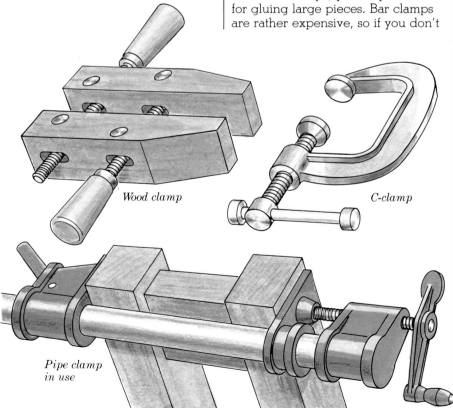

Wood clamp

C-clamp

Pipe clamp in use

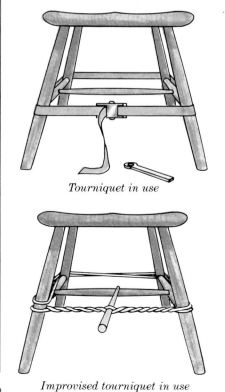

Tourniquet in use

Improvised tourniquet in use

Above: *Professional furniture repair shops have a clamp to suit every possible gluing situation. Do-it-yourselfers should buy clamps as needed, although rarely used clamps and other tools can be rented.*

Left: *To make sure that a glued joint will be strong, it must be clamped until the glue is completely dry. When clamping onto wood that will be visible, use folded newspaper or thin strips of wood to prevent the clamp from biting into the wood.*

JOINERY

Never throw away what you might need tomorrow. Seasoned wood is hard to come by; and a doweled rail salvaged from a piece beyond repair might be just what is needed for a future repair.

T*he basic methods of attaching wood pieces to each other have evolved through centuries of woodworking.*

Basic joints
There are numerous variations, but the principle is always identifiable.

Butt joint
This is when two pieces are fitted end to end or side to side and attached to each other. The butt joint is a weak joint, but it is used to fashion flat components such as tabletops.

Dado joint
Variations include the rabbet and groove. They are all made by fitting one piece of wood into a groove (or dado) cut in the other piece. This is a strong joint often used to form shelves, drawer sides, and bases.

Dovetail joint
This consists of fingerlike cuts that project from the end of one piece and fit into cutouts in another. Dovetails are strong joints mostly used to join pieces at right angles. In well-made furniture, the drawer fronts are dovetailed to the side pieces.

Lap joint
As the name implies, this is made by overlapping the end of one piece with part of another. Grooves are cut so that the boards lie flush. A full-lap joint is when the overlapped board is grooved deep enough to accept the full thickness of the lapping board; a half-lap refers to a joint where both boards are grooved. These joints make strong, neat connections.

Mortise-and-tenon joint
A mortise (slot) and tenon (tongue) joint is one of the most widely used furniture joints. It is very strong and often used to join the side rails to the front and back of a piece of furniture.

Doweled joint

A joint strengthened by cylinders of hardwood is a doweled joint. Any joint can be strengthened in this way. The use of dowels eliminates the need for screws in most situations. Dowels are often used to strengthen such intrinsically weak joints as butt joints. Tabletops, for instance, are usually made of several boards butted together edge to edge, doweled, and glued. Properly made doweled joints are usually fashioned so that the dowels are invisible. An exception to this are the dowels on extension leaves of a dining table. These, of course, become invisible when the extension leaves are fitted to the tabletop.

Doweled joints are particularly useful in repair work, when they can be used to replace more complex joints that are damaged, for example, when the tongue of a mortise-and-tenon joint has broken off. Doweled joints are frequently used at stress points, since the dowel is able to withstand stress from all angles. Dowels can be homemade or bought ready-made. Commercially available dowels come in various sizes, and all have ring grooves to hold glue.

Hardwood (usually birch) rods for doweling are available in various diameters, and dowels of the required lengths may be cut from these. Each dowel should have at least one $1/16$-inch groove along the entire length, and two may be better. (When the glued dowel is pushed into the hole, excess glue escapes up these slots; the glue does not accumulate at the bottom of the hole and prevent the dowel from going all the way in.) Round off both ends of dowel with abrasive paper, for easy insertion.

Making a doweled joint

A doweling jig is an indispensable aid in making doweled joints. The holes drilled in both pieces must be directly opposite each other, and a jig makes it almost impossible to drill these holes in the wrong places.

To make a doweled joint by using a doweling jig, begin by placing pieces to be joined side by side. Align them as they are intended to fit when joined, then clamp them together.

Use a carpenter's square to mark a straight line across both pieces at the points where the dowels are to fit. Now put the jig on one piece, sight the penciled lines through the holes, and clamp the jig to the wood. Put the drill bit through the drill guide on the jig, and drill a hole that is slightly deeper than half the length of the dowel. Markers on the jig will help you to drill in exactly the right places. Drill as many holes as needed; the joint will probably require at least two dowels. Now drill the corresponding holes on the other piece of wood. Apply a light coat of glue to a dowel, and insert it into one of the holes. Put glue-coated dowels into all the holes in one piece, and fit the other piece over it so that the dowels go into the corresponding holes. Tap the joint tight with a mallet or hammer, masking the piece with folded cloth or newspaper to prevent marks. Clamp the joint and wipe off excess glue.

Many repair jobs involve drilling out broken dowels. In the interest of accuracy, use a doweling jig for the job and proceed just as though you were drilling a new hole.

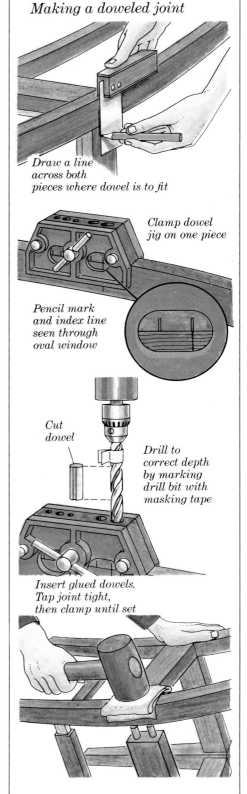

Making a doweled joint

Draw a line across both pieces where dowel is to fit

Clamp dowel jig on one piece

Pencil mark and index line seen through oval window

Cut dowel

Drill to correct depth by marking drill bit with masking tape

Insert glued dowels. Tap joint tight, then clamp until set

REPAIRING

O nce you have decided that the piece is worth restoring, inspect it thoroughly to determine exactly what needs to be done. All repair work must be completed before work on the finish can begin. Keep in mind that there is a definite order in which repairs should be made, and that working in a disorderly fashion can create all sorts of unnecessary difficulties.

Repairs are the most difficult part of any restoration project. If you doubt your ability to do repair work successfully, consider having it done by a professional. Don't run the risk of spoiling an attractive and valuable piece of furniture.

Whenever possible, loose joints should be repaired without disassembling the piece. In this case a late-nineteenth-century chair had gone beyond the point at which repairs could be made by injecting additional glue.

In general, structural repairs should be done before cosmetic ones. However, it is sometimes more convenient to attain the desired surface, such as on scored and gouged wood, before work is begun to true up a warped bed frame or make sure that drawers open smoothly.

Examination and plan of action

Begin by making a checklist of all defects. Include everything.

☐ Are there broken parts that need to be repaired?

☐ Does the piece need to be taken apart, either partially or completely, and reglued?

☐ Can veneer be repaired or should it be replaced?

☐ Are the legs of uneven lengths?

☐ Do the drawers open and close smoothly?

☐ Are there cracks, damaged carvings, burns, and gouges?

☐ Is there evidence of dry rot?

☐ Are there missing parts?

☐ Is there missing or damaged hardware?

When everything that needs to be done has been listed, plan the sequence of the various repairs. Generally speaking, major repair work should be done first.

LOOSE JOINTS

*O*ne of the most common furniture faults—especially with chairs—is loose joints. Whenever possible, solve the problem with glue. Avoid disassembling a piece unless the joints need to be strengthened and repaired or you need to remove and replace a section.

Gluing loose joints

Shaky joints can be reglued without taking the piece apart if the loose joints are not filled with dirt and old glue. The simplest way to do this is by applying glue with a toothpick and rocking the piece to work the glue into the joint. If possible, turn the piece so that the joint is vertical—that way, the glue penetrates to the bottom of the joint.

Glue may also be injected into a loose joint with a plastic squeeze bottle, a glue injector, or glue needle. Inject glue directly into the joint.

If the joint is not loose enough to accept an applicator, drill a small hole at an angle to and through the joint. The hole should be about 1/16 inch and placed where it will not show. Inject glue into the drill hole. Continue to force glue in until the overflow begins to squeeze out of the joint. Wipe off excess, clamp the joint, and let the glue set.

Disassembling joints

It may be possible to simply pull the old loose joint apart. If it is not, use a mallet or hammer (a rubber mallet is best) to break apart the glue bonds in the joints. Use a block of wood to protect the surface that you strike. A block of softwood padded with a sheet of cork is best, but a block thickly wrapped with newspaper will do quite well.

Place the protective block as near as possible to the joint to be separated, and use no more force than is needed. If possible, hold the piece up slightly with one hand (about ½ inch from the surface it is resting on) while striking downward on the block with the other.

If the glue bond doesn't break easily, don't smash it with excessive force. Instead, use a lever to pry the joint open. To make a lever, you need two narrow pieces of wood. The combined length should be slightly longer than the distance between the parts to be separated.

Cut a concave *V* in the end of one piece and shape the end of the other into a convex *V*; the two pieces should fit together. Position the two pieces so that the unshaped ends are as near as possible to the joints to be separated. Use cork, softwood blocks, or folded newspaper to pad the ends of the lever that touch the furniture. Fit the V-shaped ends of the lever

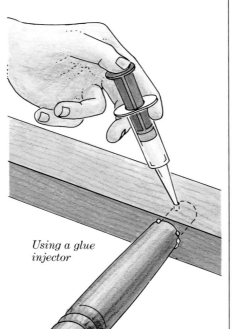

Using a glue injector

together to form a joint. Press downward on the V-joint with your hands, gradually straightening the lever and forcing the glued joints to separate.

Disassembling pinned joints

Some glued joints are pinned, and the first job is to find the pin and remove it. If you can't see the head, look for a plug or filled hole where the pin has been countersunk. Tap the pin through with a nail set or pull it out with a pair of nippers.

If the joint has been pinned with a wooden dowel and plugged, the plug should be pried out with an ice pick or an awl, or drilled out with an electric drill set to reverse. If possible, tap out the pinning dowel by lightly hammering on a dowel of slightly smaller diameter or drill out the old dowel. Use a doweling jig to keep the new hole straight.

Disassembling dovetail joints

Take special care when breaking the glue bond in a dovetail joint—the interlocking fingers of the joint will break if the force is applied at an angle. Force the joint open by striking one element of the joint so that the fingers are driven straight out.

Make a lever to pry open stubborn joints

CHAIR PROBLEMS

As a general rule, a chair should be broken down into as few separate elements as possible when making repairs on one part.

Whenever possible, repair a loose joint without separating it by gluing it as described on page 21. In order for this approach to work, the joint must be basically sound. Never ignore a broken dowel, tenon, or mortise; take the joint apart and repair it.

Types of chairs

Wood chairs are of two general types: platform chairs and frame chairs.

Platform chairs are basically stools—all the members and back elements fit into the seat. The back and leg assemblies are joined together by rungs and rails, but they do not depend on each other for structural strength.

Frame chairs are made so that the seat rests on seat rails that are part of a framelike structure formed of the leg and back elements joined.

When a chair that is in regular use develops a loose joint, repair it as soon as possible. A loose joint will very likely become a damaged joint, making the eventual repair more difficult. It will also stress all the other joints and cause them to loosen.

Chair joints

The most commonly used joints in chair manufacture are mortise-and-tenon joints, which are frequently made with dowels. In a dowel joint the end of a chair member is fashioned into a dowel-shaped round tenon that fits into a socket-shaped mortise in another member. These joints are usually just glued together, but they may be reinforced with dowels or brads driven in from the side.

Loose rung joints

Rung joints are the most likely joints in a chair to become loose. Chair rungs are usually fitted to the legs by means of round dowel joints, though sometimes square mortise-and-tenon joints are used.

If the dowel ends of a rung have shrunk with age or have been loose so long that motion in the joint has worn them down, it will not be enough simply to glue the dowel in place. The dowel end should be expanded with a wedge or wrapped with string to make a tight fit. To do this, first remove the rung from the sockets and clamp the rung in a vise.

If the dowel is only slightly loose, build it up by wrapping it with string. Tie off the string and coat it with glue.

If the dowel is very loose, cut a slot down the center of the end of the dowel with a backsaw. Shape a wedge out of a piece of hardwood and drive it in the slot with a hammer. The wedge should be just wide enough to expand the dowel end so that it will fit snugly in the hole.

Check the way the joint fits before applying glue. If the fit is as it should be, cut off the end of the wedge flush with the dowel, apply glue, and assemble the joint. Clamp the rung securely and allow it to dry. Use a pair of bar clamps or a tourniquet. (To make a tourniquet, wrap a piece of clothesline around the chair legs; tie the ends together when the rope is reasonably tight; and insert a piece of wood, such as a paint paddle or a tongue depressor, under the rope. Turn the stick until the rope is tight enough to hold the assembly in place. Lodge stick behind a heavy object to keep tension constant.)

Sometimes a dowel joint breaks off at the dowel, leaving splintered wood in the hole. Dig out the splintered wood with an awl or some other pointed tool, and glue a hardwood plug in the hole. Cut the plug off flush and follow the instructions for redoweling given on page 24.

Loose tenon joints

A loose tenon can be shimmed with thin strips of wood. Small pieces of veneer are good for this purpose. Thin strips of birch, which can be found in shops dealing in supplies for model makers, also make excellent shims. Cut a piece of shim to the exact size of the tenon and glue it to the side of the tenon. When the glue is dry, try the tenon for fit. If it is too large, sand it down with coarse abrasive paper. If it is still too small, glue on another shim and sand as necessary for correct fit.

Cracked seats

Chair seats made of solid wood sometimes crack with the grain. Flat parts of other types of furniture, such as tabletops and the tops and sides of cabinets, also crack in this way. If the crack runs end to end, separating the wood into two parts, the repair job is

Tightening loose tenon joints

Pad rung and clamp in vise

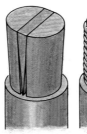
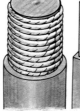

Wedged joint   *Wrapped joint*   *Shimmed joint*

relatively easy. Simply convert the crack into a dowel joint. Drill several dowel holes in the cracked surfaces of both pieces. Use a doweling jig to be sure the dowel holes match up. Insert glued dowels into one half of the piece—three or four dowels are usually enough. When these have dried in place, apply glue along the entire surface of the crack, fit the pieces together, and clamp until dry. (Use a pair of bar clamps, and attach them carefully so they do not pull the pieces out of alignment.)

Broken or missing rungs and back spindles

Chair rungs and, less frequently, back spindles sometimes develop longitudinal splits. Rungs, in particular, sometimes split apart into two pieces. Simply glue the rung back together, fitting the parts as they were originally, and clamp with C-clamps.

Replacement spindles

Sometimes one or more rungs or back spindles are so badly damaged that repairing them is difficult or impossible. When this is the case, make an entirely new part as a replacement. This is fairly easy to do if the original piece is round or square and has not been shaped in any way. Just buy a new piece of wood of similar size and of the same or a similar species as the original, then plane and sand it to match.

If the broken piece has been turned to a distinctive shape on a lathe, you will either have to shape a similar piece yourself or take the piece to a professional to have it done. If you own a wood lathe and know how to use it, making a replacement part is a simple matter.

It is possible, of course, to hand-fashion certain replacement parts, but pieces turned on a lathe are almost impossible to duplicate without a lathe. Don't try it. A professional woodworker can turn the part quickly and easily, at a reasonable price.

Chairs take a lot of punishment and, even if the finish is in good shape, they often need repair. Shaky joints, loose rails, missing slats, and uneven legs are all common problems.

WOBBLY TABLES

Tables, dining tables in particular, are subject to a good deal of wear and tear. They get dragged around, and the legs get kicked; the legs may break and become loose and wobbly.

Tables meant for everyday use are usually made with the top attached to a rectangular frame of boards, which is joined to the tops of the legs. Occasionally this frame, known as an apron, is joined to the tabletop and the legs are bolted, rather than joined, to the apron. Simple tables not intended for hard use often have the legs attached directly to the top. These joints and attachments are held together in various ways—by glue, by dowels, by bolts or screws, or by some combination of these three.

Stabilizing a wobbly table

If you have a glue injector, a single glued joint that has loosened slightly can be fixed without disassembling

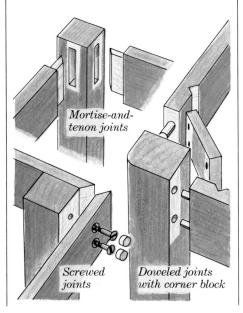

Mortise-and-tenon joints

Screwed joints

Doweled joints with corner block

the piece (see page 21). If the damage to the joints is extensive, however, you will probably have to disassemble the joints and make more extensive repairs. If one joint has loosened, it is very likely that the other joints have weakened.

To get at these damaged joints, it will probably be necessary to take the table apart. Lay a rug or drop cloth down in the work area. Turn the table upside down and place it on the rug or cloth to protect the finish on the top. If the top is screwed or bolted to the apron, remove these fasteners. If the top is held on by metal clips, unscrew and remove these.

Now look at the points where the legs are attached to the frame. If the legs are bolted on, unscrew the bolts. If they are attached by joints, examine them to see what type of joint has been used. Three types of joints are commonly used to make these attachments: lap joints, butt joints, and mortise-and-tenon joints.

Mortise-and-tenon joints

The most frequently employed joint for attaching a table apron to the legs is the mortise and tenon. Wooden tongues (tenons) on the components of the apron are fitted into slots (mortises) in the legs. The glue may dry and loosen, and either the tenon or the mortise (or both) may crack. Cracks in the top of the leg, around the mortise, may be injected with glue and clamped with a C-clamp to dry. A loosened joint may also be injected with glue. If you inject glue into a joint, use a pipe clamp running to the opposite leg to hold the joint in place.

If the tenon has cracked or has partially broken off, cut off the tenon flush with a dovetail saw or some other fine-toothed saw. Remove dried glue and pieces of broken tenon from the mortise by using a chisel. Now fashion a wooden plug of the size of the tenon and glue it into the mortise. When the glue is dry, smooth the plug down flush with the leg with a wood chisel. Now convert the joint

into a doweled butt joint, following the instructions given on page 17.

Screwed joints

If lap joints have been used, the frame is glued and screwed to the outside surfaces of the legs. The screwheads are probably countersunk and concealed with wooden plugs. Drill or pry out these plugs and unscrew the screws. Now break the glue bonds by using the disassembly techniques described on page 21. Reglue the loose joints and insert new screws of a larger diameter than those originally used. Clamp the joints securely with bar clamps or a tourniquet and allow them to dry. Conceal the countersunk screw heads with wooden buttons or plugs cut from doweling stock.

Doweled joints

Like screwed joints, butt joints reinforced with dowels are also often used to join table legs to the apron. Butt joints are sometimes reinforced with corner blocks or plates, and these should be removed before the joints are broken open. If the dowels in the joint break when the loose joints are separated, drill them out and replace them or cut them off flush and fashion new dowel joints with the dowels in new positions. Reassemble and glue the joint, screw the corner blocks or plates (if any) back in place, clamp the joint, and and allow it to dry.

Strengthening a joint

Any of the apron-to-leg joints can be reinforced with corner blocks if there is any doubt that the repaired joints are strong enough to stand up to frequent use. To do this, cut a triangular wooden block so that the grain runs from one element of the apron to the other. Notch the block to accommodate the leg. When the block has been shaped to fit, attach it to the leg with two wood screws, one driven into each side of the leg.

WARPED TOPS

Tabletops, drop leaves, and other large flat areas of solid wood may become warped. Flat areas that have no underlying support—such as cabinet doors—are particularly subject to warping and twisting.

If the top of a board is sealed against moisture by being finished but the underside has been left bare, the bottom may absorb moisture as the top dries out, and the wood cups and pulls away from the fastenings.

Kerfing the underside

Taking the warp out of a tabletop, for example, is not difficult, but it does require care and a specialized piece of equipment—a radial saw. If you have this essential tool, the first step in correcting a warped surface is to disassemble the piece so that each of the warped boards can be handled singly. Be sure to mark the pieces so there can be no confusion about how they go back together. Next check each board making sure there are no nails, screws, brads, or other metal objects. You are now ready to kerf (cut) the undersides with the saw.

Set the saw so that the blade will cut the boards to a depth of about three quarters of the thickness of the wood. Make a series of cuts on each warped board. The cuts should run nearly from end to end and be spaced about 1 inch apart. Stop each cut just before reaching the end of the board.

Place the kerfed boards on a flat surface, with the kerfs facing up, and dampen the wood with a spray bottle.

While the wood is still wet, weight the boards with objects heavy enough to press out the warp. Set the boards aside until they are dry.

To prevent the boards from rewarping, shim the cuts with thin strips of wood. Strips of scrap veneer, which can be tapped in and glued, work well.

Attaching battens

If kerfing does not completely remove the warp, attach a pair of hardwood battens to the underside of the boards. These should be a bit shorter than the width of the tabletop, at least ½ inch thick, and about 2 inches wide. Bevel them on both ends to make them less visible. Clamp the battens to the underside from 8 to 12 inches from the ends, where they won't get in the way of the legs or frame. Fasten them to the surface with wood screws. Put in the first screws at the point where the battens touch the highest part of the warp. Tighten the clamps and drive the screws successively closer to the low point, gradually drawing out the warp completely.

Kerfing the underside using radial arm saw

Glue shim strips into kerfs

If kerfing and shims do not cure the warp, screw on battens

FAULTY DOORS

Doors that don't close properly often require only minor repairs to be functional. Imperfect closure can often be solved by merely tightening the screws in hinge plates.

Occasionally, a tilted door can be rehung by slightly moving the position of the hinges. Doors should be trimmed to fit only when no other remedy is possible, such as when the frame has been twisted out of square. Sound joints should not be taken apart unless absolutely necessary—problems may multiply the more the piece is disassembled.

Doors that stick

If a door binds or sticks when you close it, the first thing to check is whether the screws in the door hinges are loose. If the screws are tight and the door still sticks, take screws out of hinges where they attach to the cabinet and remove door.

Usually there are mortises (cut-out indentations) so that the hinge leaves seat flush with the surface of the wood. Deepen the mortise for the top hinge by about 1/16 inch using a wood chisel and mallet; if there is no mortise, cut one for the top hinge to a depth of 1/8 inch.

Twisted frame

Reattach the hinge and check the door swing; if the door still binds, the problem is probably in the cabinet frame, which is very likely twisted slightly out of shape. Rather than try to bring the frame back into true, the best procedure is to plane the edge of the door.

Mark the door edge with a pencil at the point where the door starts to bind. Remove the door from the cabinet. Mark the top or bottom edge of the door (whichever is nearest the first mark) with a pencil at a point about 1/8 inch from the edge that binds. Connect the two marks with a line drawn with a straightedge. Use a plane to take the edge down to the line—take care not to remove any wood from the area where the door doesn't bind. Rehang the door, which should now fit properly.

Warped door

An imperfect door closure—that is, when part of the door won't close at all—probably means that the door is warped. As the first solution, try changing the position of the hinges.

To determine how far the hinges must be moved, measure the distance that the door misses closure at the protruding corner. Remove the hinges and insert glued dowels into the screw holes, plugging them completely. If the new holes will impinge on the old, allow the glue to dry before drilling. It may be possible to correct the bad closure by moving only one hinge, but for the best results, reposition both hinges.

To determine the position of the new screw holes, divide the distance of the door displacement in half. This will allow you to figure out how far the hinges should be moved. The hinge directly (not diagonally) opposite the protruding corner should be repositioned inward half the distance to full closure. The other hinge should be repositioned outward an equal amount. Have someone hold the door where it should be repositioned while you put pencil marks where the new screw holes should be drilled.

The problem is complicated if there is a set of double doors. Even if only one door is warped, all four hinges should be repositioned. Divide the door displacement by four and move each hinge by that amount, but reverse the direction in which you move the hinges on the unwarped door. If both doors are warped, make separate measurements and deal with the two doors separately. All this will probably be a delicate operation involving close measurement, so if you are an inexperienced worker, you may conclude that the best course is to take the job to a professional.

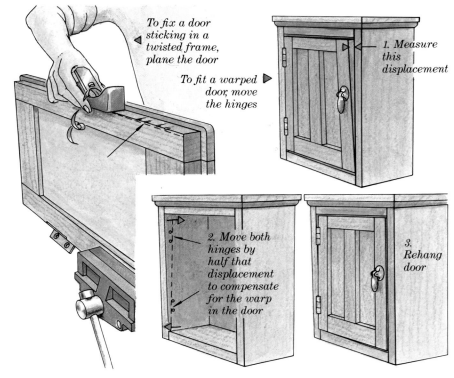

To fix a door sticking in a twisted frame, plane the door

To fit a warped door, move the hinges

1. Measure this displacement

2. Move both hinges by half that displacement to compensate for the warp in the door

3. Rehang door

Constant opening and closing of
furniture doors takes its toll. Sometimes
faulty door closure can be corrected by
merely tightening the screws or by doing
a little planing. Seriously warped doors
usually need to be rehung.

DIFFICULTIES WITH CASTERS

The shank of a stem caster fits into a sleeve inserted in the leg of a piece of furniture. Because it is difficult to match an old caster, it is usually necessary to replace all four even if only one is missing or damaged.

Casters are of two general types. Plate-mounted casters screw onto the underside of a piece with a flat base; stem casters fit into sleeves that inset into furniture with legs.

Plate-mounted casters are used on pieces with flat bases; stem casters are usually found on furniture that has narrow legs.

Not much can go wrong with plate-mounted casters, but stem casters may become loose in the stem or the sleeve. Since sleeve casters are available in various sizes, a loose caster can easily be replaced with one of a larger size.

To remove a caster sleeve, first take the roller and shaft out of the sleeve; then work the sleeve loose with a small prybar. If the sleeve can't be pulled out in this way, put a threaded bolt of about the same diameter of the sleeve down into the sleeve and tap it with a hammer until it's stuck tightly. Grasp the bolt with a pair of pliers and pull the bolt and the sleeve out of the hole. Using a doweling jig to center the bit, drill out the hole so that the next larger size caster will fit.

If the leg is too small to accommodate a larger caster, the hole will have to be filled with a dowel and redrilled with a smaller hole so that you can use a smaller caster sleeve.

Drive a new caster sleeve into the new hole by placing a block of wood on the caster and tapping the block with a hammer until the toothed flange on the sleeve is driven into the wood. Push or lightly tap the caster stem into the sleeve.

If the new caster will be visible, you will probably want to replace all the casters—even those that are not loose—with ones that match.

PROBLEMS WITH DRAWERS

Drawers that have been pulled in and out for years often develop problems. Sticking drawers are usually caused by one of the following situations.

Warped base

If a drawer sticks because the base is warped, remove the base by pulling out the tacks or brads that attach it to the drawer back and slide the base piece out. Simply reverse the base piece so that it warps upward, slide it back into place, and renail it.

Replace a base piece that has been damaged beyond repair with a thin piece of plywood. If the base is dadoed into the front and back of the drawer, disassemble the drawer.

Uneven runners

Constant use can cause the sides to wear in the places where they slide along the runners. The drawer sticks as the wood becomes uneven.

Remove the drawer and clamp it upside down in a wood vise. Plane the sides lightly, emphasizing the area toward the back, as the front is usually where most of the wear has occurred. Take off as little as necessary to allow the drawer to run smoothly.

If the strips of wood that form the runners are also worn, replace them. Cut new strips out of hardwood, glue and clamp them in place. Plane and sand the runners lightly until the fit is smooth. Lubricate runners and drawer edges with paraffin.

Typically, the center drawer guide consists of a wooden cleat attached to the cabinet frame. The cleat fits into a pair of runners attached to the center of the drawer base. These may be

planed and sanded until the drawer slides easily or replaced if necessary.

Loose joints

Pull loose dovetail and dado joints by hand or, if joints resist, knock them apart with a mallet using a block of wood to cushion the blows. Chisel all traces of dried glue from the joints.

Apply white or yellow glue to the joints, reassemble, and clamp. Check immediately with a carpenter's square to see that all angles are true. Be sure that diagonal measurements from corner to corner are the same.

For added stability, it's a good idea to reinforce the corner joints with blocks. Cut triangular blocks and apply glue to all surfaces that will come in contact with the drawer. Press the blocks firmly into place and rub them back and forth until the glue begins to develop some tack and the block starts to resist movement.

Warped or damaged bottom boards can cause a drawer to stick or refuse to close. Often the problem can be fixed by reversing the boards or by replacing them.

MISSING PARTS

*S*ince *most furniture is symmetrical, it is usually possible to duplicate broken or lost parts by copying the original opposite part.*

If the part has a simple shape with one flat surface, it can be used directly as a pattern. Often the part needed is a mirror image of the one that you will be copying; if so, the profile must be inverted. Cut the model in half lengthwise, turn one half over and use this for a pattern. However, this means that you will have to make two new parts instead of one—the second to replace the one you cut up.

Hand-cutting replacement parts

Almost any furniture part that does not need to be lathe-shaped but does contain too many complex angles to be cut out with a hand-held power saw can be shaped with hand tools. Remove the section to be copied while leaving the rest of the piece as intact as possible. Trace the outlines onto stiff paper. If the piece is complicated, make 3 separate paper patterns—1 each for the top, bottom, and sides. A straightedge, calipers, protractor, and a T square are some of the tools that may be needed to transfer the dimensions accurately. Cut out the paper profiles and transfer 1 of them to the new piece of wood. (If possible, the new piece should be made from old wood. Wood is more porous when old than new, so it will be easier to match the original color and finish.)

Clamp the piece to a work surface, and cut along the outside of the line with a knife, saber saw, or coping saw. Proceed to trace and cut the second profile and then the third.

Check frequently as you work to compare the dimensions of the new piece with the measurements of the one that you are copying.

Final shaping of detail pieces should be done with wood chisels, wood rasps, a thumb plane, and coarse abrasive paper.

Sculpting gesso replacements

It is sometimes difficult to replace broken decorative carvings with carved wood replacements.

A simple and practical alternative is to use a mixture of plaster of paris, water, and white glue to sculpt a replacement part. This mixture, known as gesso, hardens into a plasterlike substance that accepts any conventional finish. Usually it is covered with an opaque finish since it is difficult to simulate wood convincingly. (In fact, decorative detailing on most ornate, gilded picture frames is made from gesso, not wood.)

Making gesso

To make gesso, put about ½ teaspoon of plaster of paris in a pony or other small glass, and dribble in a little water and a few drops of white glue. Use water-soluble glue; ordinary white glue is best. Stir the mixture with a flat piece of wood until it reaches a consistency that can be easily worked with the fingers. The gesso must have a smooth texture to be usable; discard if it gets dry and crumbly. It takes a little experimenting to find the correct proportions of plaster, glue, and water.

Gesso sets up very quickly, so make small quantities and apply and shape it as soon as it is mixed.

Applying gesso

If the area to be repaired is large or deep, build up the patch in stages, mixing fresh gesso for each layer.

Prepare the damaged area by coating it with a thin layer of white glue.

Do this before mixing up the gesso.

As soon as the gesso is mixed, roll it into a ball between your fingers and place it on the prepared surface. Quickly shape it with your fingers to match, or approximate, the surrounding design. To sculpt the gesso to its final shape, pottery tools work best, but a variety of implements including flexible table knives, awls, and palette knives can also be used.

Allow the patch to dry for 24 hours, smooth it gently with a fine-grit abrasive paper, and protect it against moisture with a coat of shellac.

Making a mold

If the design you want to duplicate in gesso is too complex to be hand-shaped, first make a mold using undamaged parts of the carving to make the impression. Many craft and hobby stores carry molding materials including a substance used by dentists that works well for this use.

Follow the manufacturer's instructions for mixing the material and apply it over the design you wish to copy. When the molding material has set—usually 15 minutes or less—peel it off and fill the mold with freshly mixed gesso.

Allow a few hours for the gesso to completely solidify before removing the mold. Before continuing, leave it unmolded overnight so that it will harden completely.

If necessary sculpt extra detailing or modifications with a single-edged razor blade or a sharp craft knife. It will probably be necessary to carve and shape the edges so that the patch fits neatly into the damaged area.

When the fit is as exact as you can make it, glue the molded gesso to the damaged area using white glue. Fill any gaps and cracks with small amounts of freshly made gesso. Seal the patch with shellac before applying the final finish.

BROKEN RUNNERS

On some rockers the original runners are cut from straight pieces of hardwood and then steamed so they can be bent to shape.

Steaming produces a strong, resilient runner, but few do-it-yourselfers are prepared to steam-bend wood.

Other rockers have runners that are cut in a curved shape and need not be bent, but since the cuts on solid-piece runners can't follow the grain of the wood, these runners don't stand up well to the continued stresses of rocking.

A third method of making runners involves laminating three pieces of curved wood together.

Laminated runners

This is the recommended way to make a runner—it produces a piece that is strong but need not be bent.

Making a pattern

Use the side of the existing runner or pieces of the broken runner as a pattern to trace on stiff cardboard. Trace the outlines of the cardboard pattern 3 times on hardwood boards.

Place the patterns so that each of the 3 sections has the wood grain running in a different direction. If possible, avoid having short grain at the ends, as this will make the ends of the runners brittle and likely to split. When the pieces are glued together, the fact that the grain of each section runs differently will give the runner more strength than a solid piece would have. Each board should be one third the thickness of the finished runner—⅜-inch or ¼-inch boards should be about right.

Cutting out the sections

Use C-clamps to secure the board to sawhorses or to the edge of a worktable and cut out the 3 sections with a coping saw or saber saw. Support each section by hand as you reach the end of the cut so the piece doesn't splinter or fall and break.

Laminating the sections

Put plenty of white or yellow glue over the entire opposing faces of the 3 sections. Press them together, aligning them carefully. Place the glued sections between 2 longish blocks of wood—these will help to distribute the pressure evenly—and clamp the whole assembly firmly with C-clamps spaced at regular intervals. You will probably need at least 4 clamps. Allow the glue to dry for 24 hours or more before starting to sand.

Sanding and finishing

When the glue is dry, take off the clamps and blocks and level out any high spots with a wood chisel, thumb plane, and wood rasp. The bottom of the runner must be particularly even and smooth. Continue to shape with abrasive paper, starting with coarse grades and working down to fine. The glue lines in the finished runner should be barely visible. Just before the final sanding, cut the holes for the tenons or dowels that will secure the runner to the chair. These must be placed at the same distance from the ends as the holes in the original runner. Otherwise, the chair will not rock smoothly. The new runner is now ready to be attached to the chair.

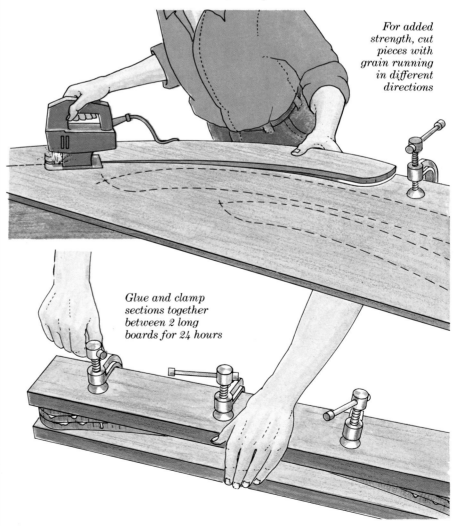

For added strength, cut pieces with grain running in different directions

Glue and clamp sections together between 2 long boards for 24 hours

BROKEN EDGES AND CORNERS

Chipped and broken edges and corners are common problems on furniture. The corners and edges of tables in particular are subject to a lot of abuse. Corners are broken off and edges become nicked and dented. Laminated tabletops may lose pieces of the top layers.

If the damage is slight, these flaws can be easily repaired by filling the damaged area with stick shellac, wood putty, or wood dough, but if the damage is more extensive, you need to cut and fit a wooden patch.

Minor breaks

A small nick on an edge or a small piece missing from a corner can be filled with stick shellac or one of the various wood composition mixtures. (Restrict the use of stick shellacs and lacquers to minor flaws because these materials become brittle when dry and tend to chip easily.) Filling is a method that can be used on both solid wood and veneered surfaces.

Build a simple form by using strips of wood, and fill it with the repair material. For minor nicks on an edge, simply tape thin strips, such as tongue depressors, on the edge with masking tape. Cut these away with a razor blade when the filler is dry.

For larger breaks and dents, use larger pieces of flat scrap wood clamped on with edge clamps, which are C-clamps designed for clamping parts to furniture edges. (Edge clamps have a screw in the deepest part of the C so that pressure can be applied parallel to the ends of the C.)

However the form is made, the inside surface should be thoroughly waxed with paraffin or rubbed with a wax crayon so the filler doesn't adhere to the form.

Fill the break with stick shellac or lacquer, wood putty, or wood dough, forcing the material into the break with a spatula or putty knife (see Deep Scratches and Gouges, page 42). If the break is a deep one, fill it in several layers, allowing time for each layer to dry before building up the next layer. Apply more filler than is needed to fill the break because the filler will probably shrink. When the filler is dry, remove the form and sand the filler flush with the surface.

Straight-edge patches

The broken corner of a solid wood cabinet or tabletop can be replaced with a piece of new wood cut to fit.

Buy a piece of wood of the same species as the original and with a similar texture and grain. The new piece should be somewhat larger than the intended patch and as near as possible to the thickness of the original.

Clear away the damaged wood on the broken corner and smooth the surface of the break until it is flat, using a wood chisel and mallet or a power router if you have one. Use abrasive paper for final smoothing. Check straightness and evenness of the corner cut with a block of wood. The block should fit perfectly flush to the corner; trim and smooth the corner cut so that it does. Cut out the broken corner until there is a flat surface running at a 45-degree angle from the 2 sides of the piece.

Cut and trim a cardboard pattern of the new corner piece. Make the pattern slightly wider on the sides so that the new piece will be about ½ inch longer than the final dimensions of the patch. (If the piece is somewhat oversize to begin with, you will be able to move back and forth to achieve the best match of the grain.) Using the pattern, cut the corner piece so the grain runs the same way as the original. Then try the patch for size, sliding it along the edge of the piece until the grain is in alignment. Mark the patch with a pencil to indicate this position and cut the wood down to size, leaving about ⅟32 inch on the sides. (The overhang can be worked down to the exact dimensions of the corner once the patch is glued in place.)

Apply glue to all surfaces of the broken corner and fit the new piece in place. A large corner patch that completely replaces a broken corner should be secured with a pair of dowels in addition to the glue. If the break goes all the way through the corner wood, the patch must be held in place with a form made of flat strips of wood. Be sure that the inside of the form is well waxed or lined with waxed paper so glue doesn't stick to it. When the form is in place, apply the glue and wedge the new piece into it. If the break is in the top or bottom layers of a laminated surface, clamp the replacement part in place with edge clamps.

Allow the glue to dry for 24 hours before removing the clamps. The fraction of an inch of overhang can now be worked down to exact alignment with the lines of the furniture, using a small plane or coarse abrasive paper. Blend the edges of the patch with the furniture edge.

Shaped-edge patches

Sometimes the broken corners will have complicated angles and curves that will be difficult to duplicate with a saw. The furniture edge may have been beveled, chamfered, beaded, or shaped in some other distinctive fashion. If this is the case with the piece that you are working on, you will find that a router will save a lot of time and aggravation.

A router is a relatively inexpensive and very handy to tool to own. Once you have used a router, you'll wonder how you ever got along without one. It consists of a motor that drives a shaping bit at tremendous speeds enabling you cut and make decorative edges. If you don't have one, you may want to rent one from a tool-rental center. The alternative is to take the damaged piece of furniture to a professional woodworker and have the patch custom cut.

If you do own a router or can borrow one, you can make the shaped edge at home fairly easily. All you need is the correct bit for the router. Sketch the lines of the shaped corner in profile. Take the sketch to your tool supplier and ask for a bit that will cut wood to match the lines of the sketch. Experiment with the new bit on a piece of scrap wood until you can use it correctly. When you feel sure of yourself, rout the edge of the patch so that it matches the other corners of the furniture.

The corners of wooden furniture—tables and cabinets in particular—are especially susceptible to damage. To make a neat repair to this post, a piece of wood needs to be fitted and glued on.

INTERIOR DEFECTS

Dents and holes in flat interior surfaces can be cut out and replaced with diamond-shaped patches.

The slanting lines of the patch will be difficult to see when the piece is finished because they will not cut directly across the grain of the wood.

Making a pattern

Make a diamond-shaped pattern out of stiff cardboard. The pattern should be large enough so that all 4 sides lie outside the part of the surface that is damaged. The easiest way to do this is to measure (with the grain) the length of the patch-to-be on the damaged surface, then measure the width (across the grain) of the patch through the middle of the first line. The 4 ends of the crossed lines will be the 4 points of the diamond. With a ruler, pencil a cross on a piece of cardboard, according to the measurements taken from the surface. Connect the 4 end points with penciled lines. Cut out the diamond-shaped pattern and place it over the damaged area, and trace the outline of the pattern on the wood with a knife or razor blade.

Preparing to patch

Now cut out the damaged area with a sharp wood chisel and a mallet. Begin by cutting lightly into the surface along the cuts marked from the pattern. Hold the chisel perpendicular to the surface and with the beveled edge facing inward, toward the area to be cut out. Tap lightly at first, gradually deepening the cuts until you have reached what you judge to be the depth of the hole or dent that you are taking out. Take care to cut the points of the diamond exactly; the cuts should not overlap.

Now take out the damaged area, working at right angles to the grain

and holding the chisel at a 45-degree angle to the surface to lift out slivers and chips. Start working holding the chisel with the beveled edge down and cutting away about ¼ inch of wood at a time. The cut-out area that will receive the patch is known as the grave. The grave should be cut out to a depth that is slightly shallower than the patch that will be placed in it. The small fraction of an inch that protrudes above the surface will be sanded down to make the surface level. (It's easy to remove extra wood, but if the grave is too deep for the patch, a new patch must be cut.)

When the grave has been chiseled out to the desired depth, go around the edge of the grave and remove the wood that is left along the downward cuts that form the outline. Now smooth out the bottom of the grave so that it is as even as you can make it.

Tape a piece of construction paper over the grave and trace the outlines with a pencil. Cut this pattern out and and transfer it to the patching wood, lining it up so the grain runs the same way as the grain on the furniture.

Inserting the patch

Cut out the patch, sawing along the outside of the pencil line with a coping saw. Again, it's better to have the patch a little too large than too small. Sand the patch carefully until the patch fits tightly into the grave. When the patch is snug, with the top surface a little above the surface of the piece, remove the patch, smear the grave with white or yellow glue, and reinsert the patch. Wipe away excess glue that oozes out the edges, and when the glue has begun to congeal, remove a little from the entire top of the crack, to a depth of a fraction of an inch. This hairline fissure will be filled later with wood putty or stick shellac so it will be invisible.

Cover the patch with waxed paper, and weight it with a stack of books or some other suitably heavy object. Allow 24 hours for the glue to dry, then fill in the edge of the patch with stick shellac or wood putty and, when this is dry, sand the surface of the patch flush with the surface of the piece.

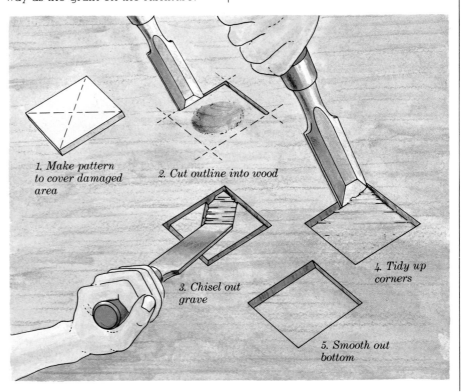

1. Make pattern to cover damaged area

2. Cut outline into wood

3. Chisel out grave

4. Tidy up corners

5. Smooth out bottom

UNEVEN LEGS

*C*hairs, tables, and other furniture with legs can be balanced by cutting off or building up the legs.

When balancing a chair or table, make sure you are working on a level surface. Tip the piece back and forth to determine which leg is the shortest.

Building up a leg

If the legs are only slightly unbalanced, the short leg or legs can be built up with chair tips trimmed to size. Felt chair tips are available at most hardware stores. If the leg is so short that a noticeable amount of felt must be used, you may wish to match the wood and make a wooden tip and attach it to the leg with a dowel joint.

Cutting down a leg

Rather than building up a short leg, you can cut down the long ones. However, you must consider whether this operation will lower the surface of the chair or table to a point where it will no longer be usable.

Balance the table by putting a small block of wood under the short leg. You will probably have to cut this block to size by trial and error. The height of the block is the amount you need to remove from the other legs. Put a block of exactly the same size against each of the other legs in turn, marking the cutting height on all faces of each leg.

Saw off the long legs on the lower side of these marks. The saw cuts must be exact or you will create new problems. Slightly bevel the edges of the cut-off legs with a wood rasp and smooth with abrasive paper. Correct any remaining imbalance with thin strips of felt glued to the bottoms of the uneven legs.

Uneven legs can be built up or cut down, depending on the severity of the problem. It may even be necessary to make a replacement part, as was done for this carved bed post.

REPAIRING VENEER

The technique of ve-
neering—applying
thin sheets of fine
wood over more ordinary
wood—has been around
for as long as recorded
history.

At one time there was a wide-
spread prejudice against veneered
furniture, which was considered
cheap looking. Actually, wood that
has been thinly sliced from a log has
a unique beauty.

Veneer is more fragile than solid
wood and more vulnerable to damp-
ness, which can loosen the glue that
holds veneer in place and cause
white discoloration (blooming) on the
surface. Veneer can also crack, warp,
break, and blister.

Whenever possible, repair damaged veneer rather than replace it—
it is very difficult to find veneer that
comes close to matching the undamaged wood remaining on a piece.

Blistering

The most usual problem with old veneer is blistering. If blistering results
from the failure of animal-based glue,
it is often possible to remove the
blister with a warm iron. The iron
simultaneously melts the glue and
presses the veneer back into place.
Use a towel to protect the surface.
Once the blister has been ironed
down, place books or other heavy
objects on the veneer, to keep it flat
while the glue dries.

If the veneer was applied with a
modern contact cement, it will probably not be possible to remove blistering with an iron. It will be necessary
either to cut through the blister, remove the old glue, and reglue or to
cut out the blister entirely and glue in
a patch.

If a blister appears in the middle of
a surface, cut it diagonally across the
grain with a craft or a wallboard
knife, using a straightedge as a
guide. Make a second diagonal cut to
intersect the first in the middle; the
cuts should form an *X*. If the blister is
on the edge of a surface, one cut may
be enough to expose the underlying
surface. Gently peel back the veneer
and use a flexible palette knife or the
blade of a craft knife to remove the
old, dried glue from the piece as well
as from the veneer. Be sure to clean
both surfaces thoroughly. Use a vacuum cleaner to remove particles. Apply contact cement to the cleaned
surfaces with a glue injector or an
artists' brush, press the veneer down,
and clean away excess glue.

Roll the repaired area with a veneer roller, which is the same tool
that is used for rolling wallpaper
seams. Gradually increase the pressure of rolling until all excess cement
has been forced out. Now place a
block of wood over the patch and
weight it with a heavy object, such as
a stack of books. Give the glue ample
time to dry before cleaning up the
surface and refinishing it.

Surface flaws

Chips, burns, gouges, and other surface flaws in veneer can be repaired
by patching. Veneer is sold by the
square foot, in strips that range from
6 inches in width to over a foot.
When buying veneer for patching,
be sure to select a piece that will be
big enough not only for the damaged
area but also for the area around it
that must be cut away. Veneer is
available in many thicknesses. Although the veneer found on most
contemporary furniture is either
$1/28$ or $1/40$ inch thick, older pieces
are often covered with veneers of
$1/20$ inch or considerably thicker.

Pieces used for patching should be
the thickest available. Once glued in
place, sand them down to the level of
the surrounding veneer. Some old
pieces have veneer so thick that
patches must be made of two pieces
of new veneer, one glued over the
other and sanded as necessary.

Choose a piece of veneer that
matches the grain of the original
piece as closely as possible. Using a
metal straightedge and a craft knife

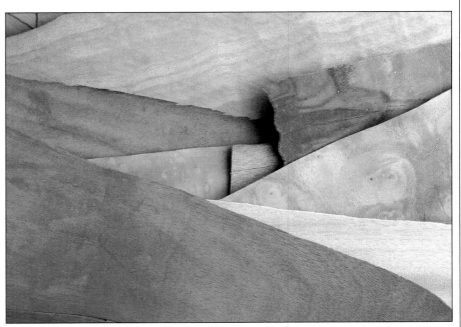

*Thin sheets of veneer have very
distinctive grain patterns.*

or a wallboard knife, cut a patch that is slightly larger than the damaged area. To avoid obvious cuts across the grain, the patch should be V-shaped if it is to go on a corner or on the edge of the surface and diamond shaped if it is to go in the interior surface. Use a series of short, light strokes to make the cut and be sure that the cuts do not go beyond the corners of the patch. Hold the knife point inward toward the patch as you cut, so that the edge of the patch is slightly beveled; the bottom surface of the patch should be a little smaller than the top surface.

When the patch has been cut out, use it as a pattern to cut out the damaged area. Place the patch in line with the grain, and trace around the edge with a pencil. This will form the outline of the grave (the cutout area that will receive the patch). Cut out the damaged area using the straightedge to guide the knife. Make the cut on the inside edge of the pencil line and bevel the knife inward at the same slight angle that you used when cutting the patch so that the grave will accommodate it as tightly as possible.

With a wood chisel held with the bevel edge downward, remove the damaged area and all traces of dried glue. If the surface under the veneer is gouged or chipped, fill it with wood putty. Let this dry before putting in the patch. Try the patch for size. If it doesn't quite fit the grave, work the edges down with a fine wood file, taking care to match the grain. When the patch has been well fitted, brush the bottom of the grave lightly with contact cement and press the patch into the grave. Wipe away excess cement and roll and weight the patch as described in the section about repairing blisters (page 36).

When the cement is dry, sand the patch down flush with the level of the surrounding veneer, using very fine abrasive paper and a sanding block, then refinish.

Match grain when making patches to repair cracked or broken veneer.

SURFACING

C an the existing finish be salvaged? Most experienced furniture restorers agree on one thing: Don't strip your piece if you can save the original finish.

The original finish on a piece of furniture can be its greatest asset. The patina, that rich mellowness that comes with age, will be lost if the finish is stripped. This affects the look and, possibly, the resale value of the piece of furniture.

If there is no way to save the existing finish, then you have no choice but to strip it off—and this is a messy business.

Test for brittleness and bad adhesion by scratching the surface with the edge of a coin. If you can scratch through the finish fairly easily, you may be able to settle for reamalgamating or rejuvenating the finish.

When all the basic repairs have been done and any loose joints have been strengthened with glue and corner blocks, work can begin on refinishing the wood.

REPAIRING SURFACES

*V*iew each defect as a problem in itself and deal with it before going on to the next. Specific defects should be handled in a certain order.

In general, overall problems such as blooming (white patches caused by moisture) and alligatoring (surface crazing) should be repaired first. One exception to this would be when a piece is to be steamed in order to take out dents. This will cause extensive blooming in the finish. Then go on to local defects, such as marring, starting with the larger dents and gouges and working down to minor scratches.

Reamalgamation

Reamalgamation is a simple technique that repairs small blemishes on shellacked or lacquered surfaces. A solvent that causes the finish to soften and spread is applied to the blemished surface. The partly dissolved finish is then brushed or smoothed with a pad.

Reamalgamation is also the best treatment for finishes that have alligatored. Alligatoring is caused by the expansion and contraction of the surface, movement that is often due to exposure to the sun.

You may occasionally find a piece on which a coat of clear lacquer was applied over enamel. Don't attempt reamalgamation on such surfaces—the result will probably be unsightly streaking.

Once solvent tests have determined what type of finish was used, clean the entire surface to remove all traces of wax and other residue. Keep the surface horizontal—the melted finish may run if it's not applied flat. The work space should be warm and dry and reasonably dust-free.

Apply the solvent—denatured alcohol for shellac and lacquer thinner for lacquer—with a brush or a soft, lintless pad. Folded cheesecloth will do, although most people find that brushing is a bit easier.

Put solvent on gently to avoid unnecessary brush or pad marks. Apply continuously, keeping the surface wet, until the finish begins to move. Stroke the damaged area to work out surface faults. When the surface is blemish-free, apply more solvent. Brushing with the grain, use light, deft strokes to brush the surface smooth.

Allow the surface to dry. Using 280- or 380-grit abrasive paper, smooth rough spots. Although the reamalgamated finish may look satisfactory, for best results apply a final coat of shellac or lacquer over the entire surface. Wait a day after applying the new coat, then sand smooth. Apply paste wax and buff.

Blooming

Blooming, the formation of white water spots, is easy to deal with. The white stain is usually fairly shallow, and light abrasion almost always takes it out. No matter which of the various rubbing methods you use, always work with the wood grain.

Sometimes a light stroking with a cloth and lemon oil works. White spots on shellac often respond to rubbing with a pad or cloth sparingly dampened with denatured alcohol, and lacquered finishes can be similarly treated with lacquer thinner.

More stubborn stains require an abrasive. Mix cigar or cigarette ashes with a little table salt, then add lemon oil, salad oil, butter, or any light oil. Rub the mixture on the spot with a cloth or a fingertip. The most resistant white spots usually respond to rubbing with pumice or rottenstone mixed in a lightweight machine oil or to 3/0 steel wool lubricated with oil or liquid wax.

Stop rubbing as soon as the spot disappears. If the heavier abrasives are used, it may be necessary to rub the entire surface around the spot to bring the tone of the finish down to match the reduced shine where the spot has been rubbed out.

Cracked finishes

The surface of furniture that stands in sunlight or near a heat source is liable to crack, craze, or check. The heat causes the wood to expand and contract, and, after a time, a pattern of cracks appears on the finish. When this pattern resembles alligator hide, the problem is called alligatoring. A maze of small crosshatches is referred to as checking.

Cracked or crazed finishes present a challenge to the refinisher; however, in some severe cases, it can be hopeless. But if the cracking or crazing is on a shellac or lacquer surface, the finish can often be revived by reamalgamation. If this fails to produce a satisfactory finish or one that can at least be used as an undercoat, the do-it-yourselfer has no choice but to strip the piece to bare wood and completely refinish.

Dents

The application of water or heat takes shallow dents out of softwoods and most hardwoods. Applying water is easy to do on unfinished pieces. Finished surfaces may need to be stripped (the dented areas, at least), although it may be possible to get enough water or steam into the wood grain by pricking tiny holes in the finish with a pin.

Squirt water over the dent and let it soak into the wood. Do this until the wood is saturated. With luck the water will raise the compressed grain and eliminate the dent. Deeper, more stubborn dents need steaming.

Soak the affected area and cover with a folded moist cloth. Briefly press the cloth with a hot iron, just long enough to produce a spurt of steam. Use the tip of the iron or put a bottle cap on the cloth to keep the iron off the wood. The steam will penetrate the wood and gradually raise the compressed grain. A few pressings over a period of 15 minutes may work, or it may be necessary to steam the wood off and on for several hours. If you had to prick pinholes in this finish before steaming, the heat will probably close them. Steaming works well on softwoods. It does not always work on hardwoods.

Taking out dents with water or steam will probably cause the finish around the dent to turn white.

Chipped edges

Chipped edges can be repaired with a stick shellac if the damage is not too extensive. On a large area, the repair may be too fragile to last.

To repair a chipped edge, make a form by taping a tongue depressor or similar strip of wood along the vertical edge. Follow the instructions given for repairing scratches and gouges (see page 42) to fill the chipped edge.

White spots and water rings

White rings from drinking glasses, vases, and flower pots are common on tables, especially if the surface is not waxed. Wax won't protect furniture from water that is allowed to stand for long periods, but it will resist it long enough for you to wipe up most spills. Shellacked and lacquered finishes are particularly vulnerable to white water stains. Varnish also turns milky in wet environments—humidity is often enough to bring up a foggy white bloom. Remove bloom by following the procedures on page 40. If the water penetrates the finish and goes through into the wood, the result is a dark stain that will be much more troublesome to remove.

Dark stains

Stains that have not bonded with the finish can be wiped away easily with a cloth moistened with turpentine or mineral spirits. If this doesn't work, superficial stains can usually be removed by careful rubbing with light machine oil and pumice. This dulls the worked area, so it will be necessary to rub the entire surface around the stain to maintain an even sheen.

Stains that have penetrated the finish, particularly ink or water that has soaked into the pores of the wood, are more difficult to remove.

Try pumice and oil first. If this doesn't work, use a very fine grade of abrasive paper to remove the finish down to the surface of the wood stain—do not rub down to bare wood. If the wood is not affected, spot refinish using matching finish applied with an artists' brush, or try padding lacquer, feathering carefully into the surrounding area. When dry, sand with superfine paper.

If the stain is in the wood but not very deep, sand down to bare wood, restain, and refinish. Don't guess at what stain to use; experiment with various stains on scrap wood until you find one that matches.

If sanding reveals that the stain is deep in the wood, try removing it with an ordinary household bleach, such as Clorox brand. Dab on the bleach with a cotton swab. Give it time to work, and neutralize with full-strength white vinegar or one cup borax mixed with one quart water. Blot up the neutralizer with paper towels, wipe the area with a damp cloth, and towel dry. If chlorinated bleach doesn't remove the stain, use an oxalic-acid solution or a commercial wood bleach, following the instructions on page 86. (Remember, these are dangerous chemicals, and safety precautions are essential.) After bleaching, restain and refinish.

Burns

Cigarette burns are one of the most common blemishes found on pieces of furniture. The repair method depends not on the type of burn but on the depth of it.

Superficial burns that have not penetrated the finish can be removed fairly easily by scraping the finish with a utility knife then sanding. Spot finish the blemish with the appropriate material.

Deep burns that have marred the wood must be scraped and filled. Use a knife blade to remove charred wood, then brush out the scrapings. If the wood around the char is discolored, it may be possible to spot bleach with denatured alcohol or a diluted solution of oxalic acid (three ounces acid crystals to one quart water). Fill the hole with a stick shellac, lacquer, or wax (see this page).

Minor scratches and gouges

Small scratches and stubborn water stains that do not penetrate through the entire finish can be removed by gentle rubbing with lubricated steel wool. Dip a pad of superfine steel wool in boiled linseed oil, baby oil, or a light machine oil such as bicycle oil. Gently stroke the damaged areas, blending in the affected spots with the rest of the finish. Stop rubbing as soon as the defect has been removed. In some cases, this gentle abrasion is all that is needed to repair the finish. The final step is to go over the surface with a tack rag and a clean cloth, apply paste wax, and buff.

Deep scratches and gouges

A badly gouged piece of furniture should be entirely resurfaced.

If there are not too many scars, however, and the holes are not much bigger than a nickel, it is possible to repair the surface without removing the entire finish.

Deep or conspicuous scratches and gouges in wood finished with varnish, shellac, or lacquer should be filled with stick shellac or stick lacquer in a shade that most closely matches the finish.

Wood dough

Wood dough consists of sawdust in a chemical binder. It is easy to work, dries fast, comes in various colors, and takes stain when it is dry. It is particularly useful for repairing broken edges and carvings because it can be built up and shaped. If wood dough dries while being worked, thin it with the product the manufacturer recommends or with lacquer thinner. Apply carefully—thinner will soften any surrounding finishes with which it comes in contact. Wood dough shrinks as it dries, so build it up in layers; let each layer dry before adding the next, and use more than it appears you need. Sand off the excess when dry.

Wood putty

This is purchased as a powder, which is mixed with water to the desired consistency. It dries faster than wood dough and doesn't shrink when dry. However, it doesn't look much like wood, so even though it can be tinted with various colors, it is best used under opaque finishes.

Latex wood fillers

Latex (alkyd) fillers are available in various colors and will accept stain. They do not shrink much and can be feathered to make a smooth transition between the patch and the surrounding wood. They do not convincingly simulate natural wood.

Stick wax

This is much easier to work with than stick shellac, and easier to find, but the results are not as durable. Use the same application procedures as given for stick shellac unless the manufacturer's instructions specify otherwise. If you patch with stick wax, you must seal the patch with shellac before touching up with the final finish material because most other finishes won't adhere to wax.

Stick shellac and lacquer

These sticks can be used to fill scratches, dents, gouges, and indentations on otherwise sound finishes. Many hardware stores carry these sticks, or they can by ordered by mail. Stick shellac is more readily available than stick lacquer and is generally preferred. The use of these sticks need not be restricted to shellac and lacquer finishes. Choose a stick that closely matches the color of the surrounding surface. Sets of sticks are available in colors ranging from beige to various shades of brown and reddish brown. Some manufacturers produce colored sticks in both opaque and transparent versions.

The instructions that follow apply to using either stick shellac or stick lacquer. If you have never used this type of product before, practice the techniques on a piece of scrap wood.

Applying stick shellac

You will need stick shellac of the appropriate color; a soldering iron; an alcohol lamp or electric hot plate; a small, flexible spatula; a sharp wood chisel or a single-edged razor blade; and some very fine abrasive paper.

Prepare the surface by cleaning out the indentation. If the area to be patched is smooth, scratch it a bit with a knife—the shellac will adhere better on a roughened surface. If you are repairing a burn mark, scrape away all charring and clean with mineral spirits. If the piece already has a finish, dab a little stain into the hole to cover the bare wood. If the piece you are working on is unfinished, stain it before you start patching.

Hold the end of the stick against the hot soldering iron and allow melted shellac to drip into the damaged spot. Let the molten shellac build up until it overflows a little.

Before the shellac hardens, smooth the surface with the heated spatula. (Don't use gas, wood, or a candle flame to heat the spatula—these will leave soot on the blade.) Press the shellac into the damaged area. If the shellac starts to harden as you work, reapply the heated spatula blade to keep the material workable. Melt and add more shellac as necessary.

When the shellac is as smooth as you can make it, let it harden. Then trim it down level with the wood surface by shaving off any excess with a sharp chisel (beveled edge up) or with a single-edged razor blade. Smooth the surface with wet, 320-grit abrasive paper dipped in a light oil. Touch up the patched area with the appropriate finish.

Stains

Removal methods vary according to the type and severity of the stain.

Superficial stains

If your piece is marred by superficial stains, you may be able to sand them out. A little test-sanding will tell you if this is the case. If the stain doesn't yield readily to sanding, give up; oversanding leaves a depression in the wood.

Stubborn stains

Stubborn stains require bleaching, which should be done before the overall sanding. For more on bleaching, see page 86.

Sometimes you can remove grease stains or other stains by spot bleaching, but this often results in an uneven coloration and the need to bleach the entire piece to even out the tone.

Food stains

Stains caused by animal fats in food that has been dropped on tables and sideboards can often be removed with commerical spot cleaners of the type used on clothes. Work the cleaner into the surface with a nylon brush, then scrub with steel wool. Repeat as necessary.

Simulating grain

Patched gouges under clear finishes will be visible as breaks in the wood grain, even when the patch is stained. A simulated grain can be drawn on the patch, using an artists' brush and colors to connect the grain lines on either side of the patch, but keep in mind that a poor simulation will look worse than a plain patch.

Holes and scars in enameled finishes and in less noticeable places on clear finishes can be filled with wood dough, wood putty, or latex (alkyd) wood filler.

Restoring the finish

Clear finishes with only minor blemishes can often be successfully overcoated once surface defects have been removed.

Most finishes that have been abraded to remove blemishes need an overcoating, however. Use a rag dampened with paint thinner to remove any vestiges of oil or wax. Brush or wipe on a coat of finish that is compatible with the first coat—that is, one that is dissolved by the same solvent. If you have any doubts that your new finish will bond with the old, make a test application in a place that won't show.

Padding lacquer is often a good choice for the new finish, as it is particularly effective in filling small defects in the surface. This material can be applied very quickly using a soft cloth as an applicator. If you cannot find padding lacquer, any compatible clear finish will do. Refer to the appropriate section for instruction on applying the new finish.

STRIPPING

Of the three methods of hand stripping—burning, sanding, and chemical stripping—only the last is recommended for home refinishers.

Burning with a propane torch, heat lamp, or electric paint remover softens the finish, which is then scraped away. This is a chancy business that will not remove wood stains, and there is always the possibility of burning the surface.

Although sanding will remove a given finish, it can be tedious and time-consuming, and there is danger of removing too much of the surface and spoiling the lines of the piece. (Wear a mask when sanding—clouds of toxic dust will be generated.)

If you think that the wood you are going to work with is old enough to have acquired a patina under the finish, then sanding is out of the question. Sanding damages the patina, at least in part, and if the patina is uneven, it will have to be removed. Removing it, though, reduces the attractiveness of the furniture and may also reduce its value. Whenever there is a patina to be preserved, use a chemical stripper.

If you know or suspect that your piece is veneered, do not even consider sanding; chemical stripping is the only method suitable for removing the finish. (Determine whether piece is veneered by checking along edges for fine lines, which indicate lamination.)

Chemical stripping is unquestionably the method of choice. It can be messy and the chemicals involved—primarily methylene chloride—are flammable, but with reasonable care

the mess can be minimized and the danger almost eliminated.

If you prefer to not do your own stripping, a professional furniture stripper will take off the old finish for a reasonable fee. However, there are disadvantages to professional stripping that you should know about.

In professional bath stripping a piece of furniture is dipped in either a hot tank bath of caustic soda solution or a cold tank bath of the solvent methylene chloride. In either case the surface of the wood—its brilliance and luster—will probably be damaged. The surface will also be roughened by the chemicals, and the wood grain will be raised. Much sanding will be needed before the refinishing can begin.

Dipped wood often takes on a gray color. Although enamel finishes are usually successfully removed by commercial methods, stained finishes often remain. In fact some stains darken as the result of tank stripping, which also draws out the natural oils from wood and may leave a crystalline deposit that tends to re-form even when wiped away.

You can avoid the undesirable effects of tank stripping by asking your commercial stripper to hand-strip your piece. A commercial stripper uses the same methods and materials that you would use, and charges you for time accordingly. If you value the piece and don't want to undertake the chore of hand-stripping it yourself, professional hand-stripping may be well worth the cost.

Chemical strippers

When shopping for varnish remover, you will find that many products are labeled paint remover. Both formulas are the same and work equally well on a variety of finishes.

The most expensive removers usually prove to be the most inexpensive in the end. They work better in every respect: They are more effective and quicker, and require less cleanup.

In general, paste-type removers

are preferable to liquid ones; they don't drip, and they don't evaporate quite as fast.

Today's paint removers are solvents that attack the paint vehicle (linseed oils in paint; resins in shellacs, varnishes, and lacquers). They won't burn or otherwise damage the wood surface, and they can be used on veneer surfaces without loosening them. (In the past lye was used to strip furniture, but this is no longer recommended. Lye tends to pulp the wood, and it is difficult to neutralize, hard to remove, and very dangerous. Some bleaches that contain lye may be useful in later finishing stages.)

Paint remover is not necessary to take off shellac; it dissolves in denatured alcohol and can be removed with a steel-wool pad. To determine whether finish is shellac, apply alcohol in an inconspicuous place.

Some removers contain wax or paraffin, which is included to retard evaporation. These removers leave a waxy residue after the finish has been taken off, and if this residue isn't removed with denatured alcohol or lacquer thinner, the new finish won't dry properly.

Wax is found only in removers specially made for use on varnished surfaces; unless working on varnish, avoid using removers that contain wax. If a remover containing wax has already been used, rinse surface with denatured alcohol or paint thinner.

Some strippers are labeled no wash, which means that they aren't thickened with wax and do not require washing down with denatured alcohol after stripping. Even if you use no-wash strippers, it's a good idea to clean with a solvent after the finish has been stripped to ensure that nothing is adhering to the bare wood when the finish is applied.

If you are considering several strippers and aren't sure which to choose, the best removers contain up to 90 percent methylene chloride.

Tools and equipment

The tools needed for chemical stripping are inexpensive, and most are already in your own workshop. You will need:

☐ a nylon paintbrush
☐ either a scraper or a broad putty knife with round corners that can be used as a scraper
☐ a paint and varnish remover
☐ a package of 2/0 steel-wool pads
☐ an old toothbrush
☐ a pair of rubber gloves (Neoprene gloves are the toughest)

A paintbrush that has been used to apply remover cannot be used again for painting. If you clean it with denatured alcohol and rinse it with hot water and soap, however, you can use it again on your next stripping project. Or you can use an inexpensive nylon brush that can just be thrown away. It's best to use a brush with a natural wood handle to prevent paint from the handle making even more mess.

Scrapers. Choose a scraper with a blade that is 3 or 4 inches wide. The corners of the scraper are probably sharp; if possible, round them off by grinding them down on a wheel. This will prevent you from gouging the wood surface, which will be softened and easier to damage as a result of stripping.

Putty knives. Putty knives that are used for stripping should have the corners or the blades rounded off to prevent scratching the wood. The quickest way to do this is with a power grinder.

Stripping is a messy and smelly business. Always work in a well-ventilated area and be sure to arm yourself with plenty of newspaper, protective glasses, strong gloves, and an apron.

In order to be able to refinish a piece of furniture properly, it should be stripped of all upholstery before you start working on it. In the case of this Louis XVI beechwood chair, that included removing upholstery from arm pads.

Preparing the piece

Clean the entire surface of the furniture before you start refinishing. This may amount to no more than dusting, but if the furniture has been stored for a long time in a garage, attic, or barn, it will very likely be dirty. Wash it down with soap and water and let it dry before you begin to strip. Furniture that has been in contact with food, such as kitchen cabinets, will probably be in particular need of surface cleanup.

Remove all hardware including hinges, casters, handles, and any removable parts such as mirrors before applying remover. (If the hardware is discolored, clean it with paint remover and spray it with clear lacquer to keep it bright before reattaching it to the finished piece.)

When refinishing an upholstered piece of furniture, you may be tempted to try masking off the upholstery with tape before using a chemical stripper. This is rarely a good idea. If the upholstery is in good condition and you want to save it, remove it or have an upholsterer remove it before you begin to work. Replace it or have it replaced when the new finish has dried completely.

Usual stripping method

Before starting, read the manufacturer's instructions thoroughly. Each product carries specific instructions—follow them to the letter. The instructions in this book can only be general.

Pour 1 or 2 inches of the stripper into a clean wide-mouthed metal can, such as one from coffee. Working with a small amount is more convenient than working from a full can and keeps the main supply free of loose pieces of paint.

Using a brush or a steel-wool pad, apply a generous coat of remover on one surface of the piece. Apply the remover to horizontal surfaces whenever possible. If necessary turn the piece as you work. This prevents remover from running down into areas where you may not want it to go—into the openings of a cabinet from which the drawers have been removed, for example, or onto bare wood, which it will stain. (If you get remover onto bare wood, wipe it off immediately with a rag moistened with denatured alcohol.) Pat the stripper on generously, brushing with the grain in one direction. Don't overbrush; use soft strokes and put on plenty of remover. Leave a heavy coat; do not brush the remover out. Continue to apply the remover onto dry spots that show up on the surface as the remover works.

Wait until the finish is soft and begins to lift before you scrape it. Paints and enamels wrinkle as they soften, and varnish blisters, but some finishes may not show much evidence that they have been softened. Test the finish with the scraper after about 5 minutes, although it will probably take from 10 to 20 minutes for the finish to become soft and movable. Test again with your scraper or putty knife when you think the surface is beginning to lift.

Don't wait for the stripping chemical to dry. Begin to scrape as soon as the finish is soft. Scrape the sticky paste off in the direction of the grain, taking care not to mar the wood, and deposit the surface material into a disposable receptacle. Be careful with the scrapings; the stripper is still chemically active and can damage anything it touches. Scrape the piece as clean as possible. Use a pointed object such as an orange stick, a sharpened dowel, a meat skewer, an ice pick, or an awl to clean the remover out of cracks, crevices, and carvings. To avoid scratching the wood, cover the point of the tool with a piece of cloth.

You may have to repeat the stripping process several times, depending on the age and thickness of the finish. With refractory finishes, it is less damaging to the wood to proceed layer by layer since prolonged contact with the stripping chemical can soften the wood to the point that the scraper will gouge. (If, when you start sanding, your abrasive paper clogs up with sludge, you need more work with finish remover and steel wool.) When you've scraped the surface thoroughly, clean up with fine steel wool, rubbing with the grain. Wipe off any remaining finish with coarse cloth (burlap is best) or crumpled newpaper.

After you have scraped and wiped as much remover and dissolved finish as possible off the surface, scrub the piece with a small brush dipped in denatured alcohol (an old toothbrush is useful for getting into cracks), and wipe the piece with a clean cloth. The final cleanup should be done with 2/0 steel wool dipped in denatured alcohol of a grade suitable for shellac thinner. For the most stubborn patches, you may need fine abrasive paper (220 grit or finer). When you are down to bare wood, use a clean cloth to wipe the piece with denatured alcohol, then dry it thoroughly with a clean rag.

When all the surfaces have been stripped clean, wipe the piece with a clean rag moistened with water, although you may be well advised to skip this step if working on especially fine wood. Water really isn't good for wood; it may stain or raise the grain. If it seems advisable to skip the water wash, conclude the stripping process with the alcohol rubdown. Let the piece stand for at least 24 hours before working on it further.

Difficult finishes

If you find a stubborn undercoat beneath the surface finish, keep applying fresh remover until the undercoat lifts. Old finishes sometimes come off layer by layer. It may be necessary to put wet cloths over the remover and leave it overnight.

Old paints—especially those made with earth, lampblack, and iron oxide pigments—can be obstinate, especially if they have sunk deep into the pores of the wood. Generously apply remover to these stubborn finishes and, while the remover is still wet, scrub the surface with a pad of steel wool. Then scrub with steel wool dipped in denatured alcohol, and wipe with a rag. Use a sharpened dowel, a knife point covered with cloth, or some other pointed tool to remove residue from cracks and corners. The surface may need to be further smoothed with abrasive paper to take off the last vestiges of finish.

Paint that has penetrated the wood can sometimes be removed by brushing on a generous coat of shellac, allowing the shellac to dry thoroughly, and using the remover in the usual fashion. The buried paint will probably come off, in whole or in part, with the shellac. Always allow stripped furniture to dry for at least 24 hours after the finish has been removed before sanding.

Stained wood surfaces

The stain under the finish coat might—or might not—come off when you remove the finish. If the finish comes off and leaves the stain intact, you can refinish over the stain. If the stain comes off entirely with the finish, you can restain in the color of your choice. But if the stain comes off only partially, leaving patches and blotches, something must be done. One solution is to apply a new coat of stain that's at least as dark as that of the original stain. Try it out somewhere that doesn't show. If this approach is unsatisfactory, you will have to bleach the surface (see page 86).

Using a spray bottle, spray the entire surface with ordinary household bleach. Repeat until all the stains are bleached out, then rinse the surface with clear water. The combination of bleach and water is hard on the wood—almost certainly the treatment will raise the grain. Therefore, use this method as a last resort only.

SANDING

Wood sanding is a must for a good finish. A thorough and careful sanding vastly improves the final finish. Never be tempted to skip this step, and do not be satisfied with hasty sanding.

Regardless of how beautiful the wood looks—whether it has never been finished or whether it is a newly stripped surface that awaits refinishing—go ahead and sand it anyway. It's well worth the trouble.

No finish can be more beautiful than the wood that's underneath it. In fact, any surface imperfections will be worsened by the finish applied on top. Woods with conspicuous surface flaws may need smoothing with a wood scraper before abrasive materials are used.

The smoothing of bare wood to a fine, silky surface is the most important step. It is accomplished with abrasive papers and steel wool. Start with the coarser grades for rough sanding and shaping; work down through the medium, fine, and very fine grades for preparatory and finish sanding; and polish with the extra- and superfine grades.

The reason for sanding is not to remove wood, though of course some wood must be removed. Think of sanding not so much as a process of cutting down wood as a process of smoothing and polishing it, of beautifying the surface so that it will only be enhanced by any finish that is applied. Do as much sanding as necessary—but no more.

There are some situations in which less sanding is more desirable, for example, with valuable antiques. A patina and the maker's tool marks add to the value of the piece, so a light hand is indicated. If you feel there is any possibility of damage through sanding, use steel wool instead of paper, or take the piece to a professional restorer.

Abrasive papers

The material that is commonly referred to as sandpaper is actually an abrasive sheet. Sandpaper is not made with sand.

A standard sheet of abrasive paper is 9 inches by 11 inches, and it is cheaper if purchased in packages of 50 or 100 sheets. It keeps indefinitely if stored in a dry place.

Waterproof abrasive papers, which are made only in the finer-grit sizes, are designed to be used with water or oil and are best used for the final rubdown when doing fine hand-sanding.

Silicon carbide paper. This is the best abrasive sheet available, though it is not always easy to find. It is available in either black or white. The only difference among the colored sheets is that the black ones are usually waterproof, for use with water in wet sanding.

Silicon carbide paper resists wear, retains the grit, and doesn't load up with wood dust. It is the preferred type for fine finishing, especially for surfaces that are to be lacquered, shellacked, or varnished.

Aluminum oxide paper. The quality of this gray sheet is good and nearly equal to that of silicon carbide paper. Available in many hardware and crafts stores, it is a superior product for most finishing projects, both for hand- and power-sanding.

Garnet paper. This garnet-colored (reddish) sheet is widely available and is the most commonly used abrasive for furniture finishing. It is of good quality, although it does not have the remarkable cutting qualities of silicon carbide and aluminum oxide papers.

Flint paper. This is the original sandpaper. It deteriorates quickly and produces inferior surfaces. Do not use if anything else is available.

Weight
Abrasive papers come in various weights and are available in two general types: open- and close-grained. The lighter weights fold easily and are useful when working in tight spots. The heavy-gauge papers are stiff and may crack when folded; use these in power sanders and whenever you need paper that will stand up to prolonged use. Open-grained papers are only lightly coated with abrasive material; close-grained ones are densely coated. Open-grained papers do not clog with granules of the sanded material, but close-grained papers work faster and more efficiently. For furniture finishing and smoothing, the close-grained type is usually preferred.

Grit
Begin with paper as coarse as the wood tolerates without scratching, then move down to finer papers until the wood is as smooth as sanding can make it. (Generally, hardwoods call for finer grades of paper than softwoods, both for starting sanding and for finishing.) To get a polished finish, this step-down procedure usually involves moving from medium to fine to superfine papers.

An effective three-step progression starts with a 180-grit (5/0) paper, moves to 240-grit (7/0) paper for the second sanding, and finishes with a 320-grit (9/0) or finer paper for the final sanding. Make adjustments in the coarseness of the paper depending on the initial condition of the piece you are working on.

Although when sanding most pieces you should begin with medium paper (120 to 180 grit), it may be necessary to use coarser paper if the surface is very rough or finer paper if the wood is exceptionally smooth. For best results always start with the finest grit size that will remove the surface defects.

Sanding blocks

A sanding block is an indispensable aid in successful hand-sanding. A sanding block holds the paper even and keeps it flat to the surface—something your fingers can't do.

Buy a block ready-made or make your own by gluing a ½-inch sheet of felt or sponge rubber around any wood block that feels comfortable in your hand. Wrap the abrasive sheet around the block and hold it in place as you sand. If you buy a commercial sanding block instead of making your own, get one that uses a quarter sheet of sandpaper and has a rubber pad between the paper and the metal parts of the block.

Steel wool

Always use steel wool instead of abrasive paper if you value the patina of the wood. Steel wool is available in hardware and paint stores in various grades, but only grades 1/0 through 3/0 are suitable for use on furniture. For most uses 2/0 is recommended. For the very fine work, such as final smoothing, use 3/0.

Steel wool can be used to remove residues of stripping chemical and dissolved finish, to smooth the wood surface after sanding and to buff between finish coats. After stripping use 1/0 grade. For final smoothing, after sanding, and for buffing between coats of finish, use 3/0.

Use steel wool with care. Too much rubbing with steel wool can polish the surface, closing off the pores so that stain cannot be applied.

As with abrasive paper, always rub steel wool with the grain to prevent scratching. Use it just as you would abrasive paper—apply straight, even strokes and keep your body lined up with the grain. Tap the wood dust out of the pads as you work.

For the very final smoothing, steel wool is superior to abrasive paper. A few whisks with a wadded ball of steel wool will pull the last traces of raised whisker up and out of the wood.

Power sanders

Hand-sanding produces the best final results, but it is time-consuming. If much finishing is required, or if the project is sizable, a power sander is a sensible investment.

Types of sanders

The most practical choices in power sanders for home furniture finishing are the orbital type and the in-line type. Both are generally satisfactory, but each has slight disadvantages.

Belt sanders, disk sanders, and drum sanders are inappropriate for the home furniture-finishing workshop. Disk and drum sanders, in particular, are poorly suited for most furniture work and may do more harm than good. Disk sanders do not provide the necessary control and can cause unacceptable scoring. Belt sanders can be used for finishing work but only with care because they are too heavy and cumbersome for most projects.

Combination orbital and in-line sanders can be useful, but they are almost twice as expensive as simple orbital sanders and for most sanding are not really necessary.

In-line sanders are for the perfectionist. These tools vibrate with the grain and do the job with the least chance of mishap. However, they operate slowly—so slowly that it's quite possible to hand-sand in the time it takes to use an in-line tool. They do not do a significantly better job than do orbital sanders. They don't leave the tiny swirl marks that orbital sanders produce when used with heavy-grit abrasive paper, but this slight advantage is offset by their slowness of operation. And abrasive papers in the grades used for most finishing projects (120 grit and finer) will not leave swirl marks if properly handled.

Sanding can be done with a block of wood and abrasive paper but a power sander makes the job much easier.

Choosing a sander

Power sanders come in various sizes. Choose a sander with a pad size most suited for the type of work you intend to do. Sanders with small pads are best adapted for fine work. A medium-sized sander is a good general choice. (Different models use different amounts of a standard abrasive sheet—a half, a third, a quarter, or smaller.)

A medium-sized orbital sander that takes one half or one third of an abrasive sheet is usually the best general choice for furniture finishing in the home. It is worthwhile to look for one that has a pad that extends beyond the sides of the sander—this feature makes it easier to use the tool when sanding into corners.

Sheets of sandpaper cut to the exact dimensions needed are available for many power sanders, although cutting standard sheets to size is not a difficult chore. (Fold the paper to size, crease it firmly, and cut along the edge of a steel ruler.)

Many sanders are equipped with a vacuum-bag attachment, as either a standard or optional feature. Sanding is a dusty business, and these attachments are recommended.

Using a sander

If you decide to use a power sander, be sure you're familiar with how it operates before starting work on anything of value. Practice on scrap wood if you're not familiar with the tool. Power sanders, even those with vacuum attachments, throw out a lot of wood dust. If you find you are inhaling this dust, wear a dust mask. (These are normally available in paint and hardware stores.)

Turn the sander on only after it is firmly in contact with the surface. If the sander is running before you bring it down to the surface, you will probably cause some marring.

The weight of the sander plus the natural weight of your hand as it guides the tool is all the pressure that should be used. Do not press down on the sander while it is working; let the weight and motion of the sander do the work. To avoid making ruts, keep the sander moving, guiding it in a straight line. Do not attempt to sand with it, as you would with a hand-sanding block. This will only produce unwanted ridges and swirls.

Power sanders are helpful for the first sanding and may also be used for the second, but for the finest results, do the last sanding by hand.

Many pieces of furniture have areas that will be difficult or impossible to reach with a power sander; therefore, some hand-sanding will probably be needed. This will also be the case when you are working on curved or detailed surfaces.

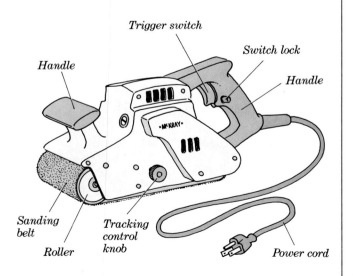

Orbital sander

Handle · Switch · Handle · Clamp · Power cord · Abrasive paper · Pad

Belt sander

Trigger switch · Switch lock · Handle · Handle · Sanding belt · Roller · Tracking control knob · Power cord

Sanding techniques

Read through the following pointers and familiarize yourself with these tricks of the trade.

☐ Always sand with the grain in straight, even strokes. You will tear the wood fibers if you go against the grain. The only exceptions to the rule of sanding with the grain are if you have trouble sanding out ridges and if you must remove superficial stains. In these cases it is helpful to sand at a slight angle to the wood grain. Remove diagonal sanding marks with finer paper during the next sanding.

☐ If you are hand-sanding, you may have a tendency to move the paper in arcs. Never work in a circular motion; keep the paper moving with the grain. Line your body up with the grain as you work.

☐ If your project requires a lot of sanding, wear a dust mask to prevent inhaling wood particles. Wearing a mask is particularly important if you are using a power sander.

☐ Sand evenly over the entire surface, taking care to make the piece uniform in texture and tone. As much as possible, keep your working surface horizontal, turning the piece as necessary.

☐ After the first complete sanding, go over the piece again with fine paper (280 grit is about right), then go over it again one final time with finer paper. Run your fingers over the wood from time to time to test for roughness. Each sanding will improve the finish noticeably.

☐ If you are hand-sanding, be sure to apply even pressure to the sanding block. Use a light hand; do not force it. Most people have a tendency to use extra pressure on the sanding block as they approach the edge of the area being sanded. Keep the pressure even to avoid tapering the surface downward. From time to time tap or brush the dust out of abrasive paper with an old toothbrush.

☐ To keep edges true and corners square, use only fine grades of paper when sanding the edges of tabletops and similar surfaces.

☐ In tight, curved surfaces and grooves, use abrasive paper wrapped around a wooden dowel. To make the paper flexible enough to wrap around the dowel, dip the paper in turpentine.

☐ Sand difficult-to-reach areas, such as the spindles in a chair back, with narrow strips of abrasive paper worked in a back-and-forth motion, like a shoeshine cloth. Narrow strips used for shoeshine-style sanding have sharp edges that may leave marks, so use them with care.

☐ Molded edges and carved surfaces, decorations, and designs are best sanded by gently scrubbing the area with a wadded piece of used abrasive paper. Follow this by scrubbing gently with fine steel wool.

☐ Be sure to sand off any glue that has oozed out of joints and dried on exposed areas.

☐ When sanding veneer, favor the edges by sanding away from them to avoid chipping them.

☐ If you are planning to use a water-based stain, dampen the wood slightly with a rag moistened with water, and let the wood dry before the final sanding. This will cause the grain to raise slightly. Smooth this feathered surface with the final, very fine sanding.

☐ If you choose to sand with water as a final sanding step, use waterproof paper (only available in finer grit) and sprinkle the surface lightly with water before sanding. For an extrasmooth surface, use light machine oil or lemon oil instead of water. After this last wet sanding, wipe the surface thoroughly with a dry, clean cloth. Water is the number one enemy of wood, so always dry the surface immediately after wetting it.

☐ Softer woods pose a special sanding problem. As you sand, the surface smooths out and then begins to fuzz. Use a sanding sealer to deal with this problem. Spray or brush on the sealer and let it dry. This will stiffen any tooth (splintery projections) making it easy to remove in the next sanding step. It also prevents any further fraying of the surface. Commercial sanding sealer is a thin lacquer, but you can formulate your own by mixing a very thin shellac.

☐ Use a tack rag between sandings to remove wood dust and stray pieces of abrasive grit. Buy tack rags, or make your own by soaking a rag in a solution made from 1 part turpentine and 3 parts varnish and letting the cloth dry.

Take care to pick up all sanding dust (if it isn't removed before finishing, it tends to make the new finish granular). When you've finished sanding, wipe the piece down again with a tack cloth.

☐ With some hardwoods it's possible to go beyond sanding to the point of polishing the surface to a slick finish; the pores of the wood seal and the surface will not accept stain as well as you might wish. With hardwoods do not use extra-fine paper.

☐ Do not let the piece stand for too long after the final sanding before applying the finish. Bare wood absorbs moisture from the air that shows up as discoloration in the stain.

Checking the surface

Locate rough spots by putting your hand in an old nylon stocking and stroking the surface. Whisk spots anywhere the stocking catches with fine steel wool.

Another good method of checking for slight surface imperfections that your sanding may have missed is to hold up the piece at an oblique angle to a bright light placed in front of you. (A bare light bulb is best.) With a little practice you will learn to find flaws by viewing wood in this way.

WOOD FILLERS

To get a smooth finish, you must start with a smooth surface. Many woods are naturally smooth, but others—such as oak, maple, mahogany, and chestnut—are open-grained. No amount of sanding will take them down to a glossy surface.

Fillers are used on open-grained woods to close the pores and fill the tiny craters and crevices that resist sanding. The filled surface is then sanded one final time before the finish is applied. Fillers may be put on either before or after the stain, depending on the effect desired. If the wood is to be sealed, the filler should almost always be applied after the sealer and before the finish coat. However, a second coat of sealer may be applied to the filled surface if the piece is to be varnished or shellacked. This wash coat of sealer consists of a thin solution of the intended surface finish.

Contemporary tastes no longer dictate that every piece have an immaculate surface. Nowadays the look of natural wood is widely preferred. Many people feel that oak and other coarse-grained woods look too slick when fillers have been used. Therefore, when working on open-grained wood, fill the grain or not, depending on your taste. If you do decide to fill, use either of the following two ways.

Method 1. The first method is to use the same material as both the filler and the finish coat.

Apply repeated coats of the finish and sand between coats. Sanding removes the finish from the high spots and leaves it in the low spots. Repeated applications and sandings build up the low spots and produce a smooth surface. If the piece has been stained or sealed before filling, take special care not to sand too much, or you will remove some of the stain or seal and cause uneven coloring.

This method is time-consuming, but it will eventually produce a glass-smooth finish. Speed up the process considerably by using a sanding sealer, which fills as well as seals.

Method 2. The more usual and preferred way to fill is with commercial wood fillers. Available in paste and liquid forms, they are brushed on the finish, then scraped off. Scraping leaves the filler in the low spots.

Liquid fillers

Liquid fillers are easy to use but suitable only for projects that require relatively little filling. Simply brush them on and sand them off.

Paste fillers

The best fillers contain a varnish-type material as a vehicle for the inert materials rather than a drying oil such as linseed oil. Hard-drying fillers give good results—so good, in fact, that many finishers find that the results achieved with soft fillers aren't worth the work of applying them.

Paste fillers are used on surfaces that require extensive filling. These fillers usually contain gypsum or silex, a form of silica. They are neutral in color and must be tinted by adding pigments after thinning.

Applying paste filler

Paste fillers are too thick to be satisfactorily applied straight from the can; thin them before using with turpentine naphtha, or benzene. Follow the instructions on the container.

Thin the paste to a creamy consistency, then add pigments specially formulated for use with your particular filler. The pigments are available in colors to match the wood or stain.

Apply the thinned and tinted filler with a stiff brush, working with the grain for the first coat. Use the brush to press the filler down into the grain. Then, while the filler is still wet, apply a generous second coat, brushing across the grain this time.

When first applied, filler looks wet. Watch it closely. Quite suddenly, it begins to look dull. This is the time to scrape it off. Don't wait; work quickly. Filler sets up fast, and if left too long it will be too dry to scrape. Scrape slightly across the grain. The idea, of course, is to take off all the excess filler, leaving just enough to fill the irregularities on the surface. A putty knife makes an ideal scraper, but any similar tool will do—even a piece of stiff cardboard.

When you've scraped the surface thoroughly, go over it with a piece of rough cloth (burlap is recommended). Burnish the surface with the cloth, working against the grain in a circular motion. Then, working with the grain this time, use a smooth, clean cloth to remove smears. Let the filler stand overnight. You may find that a second coat is necessary to level the surface. Oak, in particular, may need two applications of filler. Note that no filler can smooth the wood entirely—the finishing material is supposed to do that. Allow each layer of filler to dry for 24 hours in a warm room.

When the surface is satisfactorily filled and the filler has dried, sand the surface smooth with a fine abrasive—a piece of 4/0 steel wool is about right. Work with care. If you rub through the sealer in places, leaving blotchy patches, you will have to apply a second coat of sealer.

SEALING

Wood seal is a coating applied either before or after the application of stain or any other more-or-less transparent finish.

Reasons for sealing

When applied before the stain, the purpose of a sealer is to partially or completely seal the pores of the wood, preventing uneven absorption of the stain.

The first coat of finish is often thought of as the sealer coat, and most soft woods should be sealed with a specially formulated wood seal before a stain or any other kind of finish is applied. Fir, in particular, must always be sealed. The sealer tames the wild grain of fir so that the subsequent coating of stain goes on evenly.

Before staining

Stain tends to penetrate any soft wood unevenly, leaving the surface streaked and blotched if sealer is not applied first. (If you have any question as to whether the wood you are working with is a softwood, press your fingernail into it in an inconspicuous place; if the wood indents easily, it's a softwood.) Wood sealers even up the absorption ability.

Hardwoods usually don't require a sealer coat unless there are open-grained areas such as edges, sides, and knotholes. These should be sealed before finishing.

Before final finish

To prevent the stain from bleeding into the finish, sealers are also frequently applied after staining and before applying fillers and the final finish coat. If necessary, apply a second sealer coat over the filler.

Commerical wood seal is a colorless formulation of polymers and resins, which enhances the natural qualities of the wood. If you intend to put a final finish over the stained wood, you can mix your own sealer by diluting the finish coating with denatured alcohol or turpentine in a proportion of 3 parts solvent to 1 part finish.

Apply only one coat of sealer. Work with the grain, turning the piece as necessary to keep the working surface horizontal. Brush the sealer on thin so that it leaves no shine. Smooth with 3/0 steel wool after it has dried. If you use a commercial preparation, follow the manufacturer's instructions.

Under varnishes. Under varnishes or finishes that contain varnish, use a mixture of 1 part varnish with 1 part turpentine. Shellac sealers also work well under varnish. (If the varnish you intend to use cannot be cut with turpentine, it is a synthetic product and does not require a sealer.)

For use under varnishes and other clear finishes, many refinishers prefer commerical sanding sealers. These products are easy to apply and contain sanding agents that facilitate the smoothing process.

Under shellac and lacquer. To prepare a sealer for use under shellac and lacquer finishes, mix 1 part of 4-pound cut white shellac with 8 parts denatured alcohol.

Take your cue from a well-organized professional. A neat workshop can save a lot of time and aggravation.

STAINING

You may decide that you are unsatisfied with the natural color of the wood you intend to finish. Or having bleached a piece of furniture that had darkened with age or had otherwise become discolored, you may find that the new surface is too light. In either case the bare surface needs staining before you apply the finish.

The main reasons for staining wood are to change the color to suit your taste and to bring out the detail in woods that are not heavily grained. Staining should highlight the grain—not hide it. If it is very obvious that the piece was stained, the right stain was not used. The color should improve the general appearance or make an undistinguished hardwood resemble cherry, mahogany, or walnut. Stains are also used to simulate the patina of old wood. Certain woods, for example mahogany and walnut, have such a highly desirable color that they really shouldn't be stained unless bleaching has removed the natural color.

The best stains are formulated to bring out the full beauty of wood, not to change the natural character. To get the desired color, always consult a color chart, and try out a new stain on a piece of matching scrap wood before spreading it all over a valued piece of furniture. Remember, wet color is different from dry color; most stains dry a bit darker than they appear when first applied. Allow a test application to dry before deciding that the color is satisfactory.

Begin staining on the underparts of your piece. If you do the least conspicuous parts first, you can change your procedure if you don't like the result you're getting. Remove stain with a moist cloth and the thinner recommended by the manufacturer.

Even a clear finish darkens any wood somewhat and brings out the grain, so consider carefully whether your project really needs staining. Woods with little natural color, such as poplar, white pine, and basswood, are usually stained. Other light-toned woods—such as oak, maple, chestnut, birch, ash, and beech—may be stained or not, depending on taste. Veneers are usually not stained, nor are such deep-toned woods as cherry, mahogany, maple, walnut, teak, and rosewood.

Another question that comes up in relation to staining is whether the final finish will interact successfully with the stain. If you intend to finish your piece of furniture with lacquer or shellac, never use a stain with a linseed-oil base—the two coatings will never bond well. The surface finish is almost sure to flake away in time, no matter how well the linseed-based stain has dried.

A good way to determine the compatibility of a stain with the intended surface finish is to read the labels. If the two products do not contain a common major ingredient, the final result will be poor. Another way to ensure compatibility between a particular stain and finish is to check whether both products can be dissolved with the same thinner. If they cannot, they should never be used together. Ask your paint dealer if you are unsure about compatibility.

Every stain changes color as it dries and looks different on different woods. There are many stains on the market and many techniques for staining. All the numerous stains that are now available were developed to overcome the deficiencies of previous ones. Unfortunately, the number of choices tends to confuse the refinisher, who is looking for just the right stain for a given project. To simplify the process of choosing a suitable stain, this book discusses only those stains that result in a successful finish even when used by inexperienced refinishers. The types that fit this requirement are: pigmented oil, penetrating oil, water-based, non-grain-raising, and jelled wiping stains.

Pigmented oil stains

These stains consist of pigments suspended in oil. They work best on softwoods and tend to hide more of the grain than do other stains. They are primarily used to disguise the grain of undistinguished wood. Sometimes called wiping stains, they cover the surface with a colored film and penetrate the pores of the wood. If a piece of furniture is made of different woods, these stains can make them all look similar.

When buying a pigmented oil stain, it is important to look for the word *wiping* on the label. Some of the older types on the market are meant to be brushed on and it is difficult to achieve an even stain with these products. Check the manufacturer's instructions on the label and stick to the type that is made to be wiped on with a cloth.

The pigments in oil-based stains tend to accumulate in any imperfections in the wood, making the irregularities more noticeable. They work fairly well on hardwoods that do not have a noticeable grain but do not produce satisfactory results with

Dissimilar woods can be stained to achieve a coordinated look. Always be sure to use compatible products when thinning, adding color, and applying the final finish.

open-pored hardwoods such as oak and mahogany—the pigments tend to clog the pores. The use of these stains darkens softwoods considerably because the wood absorbs the pigment. Hardwoods, however, absorb less pigment and won't darken so dramatically. If you find that the pigmented oil stain you've chosen is too dark, lighten it gradually by adding small amounts of turpentine.

Pigment stains contain the same type of pigments used in paints but in a much smaller concentration. Although they do not change the color of the wood, they leave a film of color even after thorough wiping. Burnt umber, Vandyke brown, and raw and burnt sienna are the colors that are most commonly used; the depth of color can be controlled by the amount of wiping.

Many refinishers believe that for a piece to have a truly beautiful finish, the wood grain must remain readable. Wiping stains can obscure the character of the grain, so refinishers dilute stain with turpentine so they can apply it in thin coats. Some of the excess can be wiped away, but it's much easier to build up a finish that is too light than to try and lighten a finish that has darkened beyond the desired tone.

Pigmented oil stains have the added advantage of not raising the grain of the wood. Although they do not yield the clarity and satiny quality that is desirable for the finest woods, they have a definite place in the home workshop. In fact, pigmented oil stains are the preferred choice for many projects, particularly if the wood to be finished is not of fine quality or grade.

Penetrating oil stains

Penetrating oil stains are easy to use, do not raise the grain of the wood, and produce excellent results, especially on hardwoods. They allow more of the grain to show through than do the pigmented stains. They are particularly suited to coarse-grained woods—oak, walnut, mahogany, and chestnut—since they will not clog open pores of such woods.

Very often woods stained with penetrating oils need no further finishing—as penetrating stains produce a transparent finish that is flattering to good wood. Penetrating oil should, however, be coated with a sealer before varnish is applied over them as they have a tendency to bleed through varnishes.

Penetrating stains contain no suspended pigments; the coloring agents are aniline dyes in liquid form.

The main disadvantage of penetrating stains is that, once applied, they are difficult to remove. If you feel secure that the stain you have chosen is just what you want, this poses no problem. Be aware, though, that once applied these stains can be removed only by deep sanding.

Almost all stains contain either a dye or a pigment. Stains made with dye fade quickly when exposed to ultraviolet rays, so pieces stained with dye-based products will gradually lose their tone if placed in sunlight.

Apply penetrating stains with a brush, stroking with the grain. Let the wet surface stand for 15 minutes, then wipe with a sponge or clean cloth to remove excess stain. Depth of color can be controlled by wiping sooner or later than the 15-minute waiting period. Never allow these products to completely set on the wood before wiping, however.

Water-based stains

These stains are best used on new wood. Wood that has been previously finished usually does not accept water-based stains as well as might be desired. Even after sanding, remnants of the old finish may interfere with adhesion of the new finish.

Water-based stains are made by mixing aniline dyes with hot water. Since they contain water, they will raise the wood grain; therefore, expect to do some additional sanding if you use them.

Brush the stain on the surface and continue to add successive coats until attaining the desired color. Three or four applications may be needed, and it may be necessary to allow as much as 24 hours for the stain to dry before applying another coat.

Water-based stains can be diluted to any shade you desire. Once made they can be intermixed to produce colors that closely match a particular wood. They produce clear, vivid colors and do not require sealer coats before the final finish, although a light sealer does improve the quality of the surface. Apply the sealer after the resanding that will be necessary to take down the raised grain. A water-based stain that matches is especially effective on mahogany, cherry, or walnut.

This type of stain is compatible with any type of finishing material and is more economical than most other stains. Even after they are mixed (the usual proportions are 1 ounce of powdered stain to 1 quart of hot water), they can be bottled and kept indefinitely. They are nonfading and odorless, they wash easily off hands and equipment, contain no flammable materials, and are permanent. To apply a water-based stain, first dampen the wood with a wet sponge to raise the grain. When the surface has dried, sand lightly. This procedure minimizes the amount of grain that the stain will raise. Working with the grain, brush on the stain using long, even strokes. Shake out the brush and rebrush until the surface is covered evenly and the brush picks up the excess.

Immediately after brushing, wipe the surface lightly with a clean cloth to even out the color and eliminate streaking. Alter the shade of water-based stains by varying the amount of water and the number of coats. These stains allow almost perfect control of color. It's important, however, to avoid applying the stain unevenly—overcoating may darken an area.

Non-grain-raising (NGR) stains

These stains contain the same aniline dyes that are in water-based stains, but in non-grain-raising (NGR) stains, the dyes are dissolved in an alcohol- or petroleum-product base. This minimizes the grain-raising that results from using water. Despite the assurance of their name, NGR stains may lift the grain a little if they are brushed on rather than sprayed, but the problem is usually slight.

NGR stains work best on close-grained woods such as birch and maple. They produce especially attractive results on oak. They can be used to good effect on stripped pieces, but they work even better on new wood.

Many water-based stains can be converted to NGR stains simply by substituting denatured alcohol for water when making up the stain. If purchased already prepared, NGR stains are somewhat more expensive than water-based stains.

NGR stains are not as brilliant as water-based stains, and they tend to dry darker than their water-based counterparts. Two or three pale coats produce better results than one heavy coat. In addition, they are not as easy to control as water-based stains since they dry much faster. Therefore, it is especially important to

practice on matching pieces of scrap wood before starting on your project. After brushing on these stains, be sure to wipe the surface immediately with a clean cloth.

NGR stains are ideal stains to use under French polish. They penetrate deeply and work especially well on oily or hard fine-grained woods. They do not work well on softwoods.

Because of their fast-drying properties, NGR stains may be difficult to brush on, but when sprayed they go on evenly and will not raise the grain at all. The use of a spray gun with these stains is recommended.

Jelled wiping stains

These products have been developed quite recently to meet the needs of do-it-yourselfers and are considered to be foolproof. They work very well for projects that are not intended to look like fine professional work. When applied with a cloth or pad, there is a minimum of mess because the stain can't splatter or splash. They allow complete color control and are ideal for small jobs.

Simply rub on the stain until the surface is even; then allow to dry.

Staining tips

☐ In achieving the best staining results, the most important step takes place before the stain is applied. This step is sanding. Be sure that the wood surface is sanded as thoroughly and smoothly as possible. Stain magnifies any surface imperfections.

☐ Most furniture has sections with visible end grain. Always use a sealer on end grain, regardless of the type of wood you are working with. Otherwise end grain absorbs more of the stain than do other areas and darkens more than does the rest of the wood.

☐ Softwoods always absorb stain somewhat unevenly unless the entire surface is sealed.

☐ The only place it is acceptable to apply stain unevenly is on carved areas. After staining, wipe the high areas of carvings with a clean cloth to lighten them a little. This will throw the contours into relief, giving the appearance of age.

☐ For most stains a sponge or a folded square of cheesecloth is a better applicator than a paintbrush. But if the manufacturer's instructions call for the use of a brush, use a brush. Do small areas at a time,

always applying with the grain and pressing lightly to work the stain into the wood. Keep a clean cloth handy to pick up excess or to lighten the stain with solvent or, where applicable, with water.

☐ Whenever it is practical, turn the piece of furniture so that you are working on a horizontal surface. Keep turning the piece as you work. If you must apply stain on a vertical surface, do so from the bottom upward. This will allow you to catch any runs or sags.

☐ Begin staining in inconspicuous places. If the stain is the wrong shade or not producing the effect you want, it will not be too late to stop staining and start bleaching the affected area.

☐ Always be sure the stain is thoroughly dry before applying the finish coat. For water-based stains, drying time may be 12 hours or less, but with all other stains 24 hours is the usual drying time.

☐ When the stain is completely dry, go over the surface lightly with very fine abrasive paper or steel wool to take off any slight imperfections, including dust that may have settled during the drying time.

FINISHING

O nce your piece of furniture has been stained, you are ready to apply a finish coat. You should realize that, even if you apply a clear finish, the end result will be a color that is a shade darker than the underlying stain. If the finish coat does have color, the final look will be even darker. Bear these facts in mind when choosing both the stain and the finish, so as to prevent the piece from being darker than you want it to be.

Quality and condition of the wood have a bearing on the choice of a finish. In general, reserve the use of clear finishes to pieces that are made of wood with interesting texture or highly figured grain patterns. Dull woods or wood products are best given an opaque finish.

The type of finish needed on a particular piece depends on preference, ease of application, and the amount of wear a surface will receive.

CHOOSING A CLEAR FINISH

When choosing a finish, make sure it suits the style of the furniture and looks authentic. A high-gloss varnish on this Stickley piece would be inappropriate.

For furniture made out of high-quality, beautifully grained wood, the best finish is usually a clear one. The traditional types of transparent finishes are varnish, shellac, lacquer, oil, and wax.*

Except for shellac, these formulations are rarely natural; most of the available products are synthetic. Chemists have not yet produced a synthetic shellac that approaches the characteristic gloss and sheen of the natural product, which is based on a resin derived from insects.

Each of the clear finishes exists in a variety of types and formulations and can be used in many combinations. Shellac, for instance, is frequently used as a base coat for varnish. Choices must be made between clear or orange shellac, natural or synthetic varnishes and oils, and spraying or brushing lacquers. Each has particular qualities that affect appearance, practicality, and ease of application. Shellac and varnish bring out the grain of wood; lacquer produces brilliant, mirrorlike surfaces; wax gives a deep mellow finish that can't be duplicated by any other material. Varnish is most commonly used; shellac has great beauty but little durability; lacquer dries within seconds; and oil finishes may take weeks to dry. Some finishes may be used on both indoor and outdoor furniture; others are intended for indoor use only.

The do-it-yourselfer confronting a piece of furniture that merits a clear finish should look through the following sections before making a choice. Although personal taste is the most important factor when it comes to selecting a finish, keep in mind the type of wood to be finished, intended use of the piece, and quality of the wood and workmanship.

VARNISH

Varnish, often the best choice for finishing or refinishing a piece of furniture, is the most popular choice.

The term varnish refers to a diverse group of clear and durable wood finishes. Varnish highlights wood grain and resists water, alcohol, and heat. It produces a tough finish and is relatively easy to apply.

Varnishes are available in high gloss, medium gloss, and satin and flat finishes. A satin finish is most widely used and is the preferred choice for older pieces of furniture. The richness and smoothness of a finish are determined by the number of coats applied.

A varnish is one of two general types: natural or synthetic. Synthetics are less elastic than traditional formulas, and a few purists think that they do not rub down quite as well. Synthetic varnishes have few of the disadvantages of natural-resin varnishes, however, and they are the recommended choice.

Natural varnishes

Modern synthetic varnishes have almost completely superseded natural-resin formulations. However, varnishes made with natural resins are still being manufactured in limited quantities for specialized cases in which the goal is a simulation of period authenticity. These old-style varnishes generally consist of shellac mixed with turpentine and linseed oil in various proportions. The different formulations were named according to the intended use—spar varnish, carriage varnish, bar-top varnish, and piano varnish, for example.

Varnishes with larger amounts of oil are slow drying but more durable and flexible. They are intended for outdoor furniture or pieces that will be heavily used, such as bar tops.

The formulations intended for furniture contain less oil and produce fine hand-rubbed finishes. They dry hard and fast but are brittle and easily scratched.

Synthetic varnishes

There are four types of modern varnish formulations: vinyls (plastics), alkyds, phenolics, and polyurethanes.

Vinyl coatings

Many refinishers do not think of vinyl coatings as varnishes. Generally referred to as plastic finishes, the characteristics of vinyl coatings are different from those of the other three types of synthetic varnish. They dry very quickly (sometimes in only 15 minutes), are absolutely clear, and do not change color after application. Although they are suitable for wall paneling, they are not generally recommended for furniture finishing because they scuff and scratch easily and do not rub out well.

Alkyd-based varnishes

These products are inexpensive and produce attractive hand-rubbed finishes in warm, glowing tones. However, even the clear formulations tend to darken wood and to dry with a distinct yellow tone, which is why alkyd resins are generally used in colored varnishes. This type of varnish is sufficiently durable for most needs, although it is not as hard wearing as a polyurethane varnish.

Phenolic varnishes

The contemporary version of spar varnish, a phenolic varnish is very tough and weather resistant and is intended for exterior surfaces or garden and patio furniture. It darkens wood and dries rather slowly with a yellowish cast that becomes yellower as time passes. Even when dry, these varnishes remain slightly soft to accommodate the shrinking and swelling of weather-exposed wood.

Polyurethanes

A polyurethane finish is the recommended varnish for most furniture. Polyurethanes brush on more easily than the other types of varnish, and they dry faster than the alkyds and phenolics. Although they do darken wood at the time of application, they don't darken after application and are the clearest, least yellow of all varnishes.

Polyurethanes also resist abuse better than other synthetic varnishes. In fact, they are among the toughest finishes that you can put on furniture and are particularly well suited for pieces that are intended for high-wear situations such as tabletops and bar tops. This does not mean you should restrict their use to pieces that will have to take hard knocks. Polyurethane finishes rub out nicely to a beautiful, water- and alcohol-resistant finish and are available in a complete range of finishes, from deep gloss to flat.

Although polyurethanes are the best and most versatile of the synthetic varnishes for general furniture finishing and refinishing, never apply them over shellac. These finishes are incompatible; a shellac undercoat causes a polyurethane finish to cloud.

Remove all knobs, handles, and any hardware before either stripping or finishing a piece. Strip or clean the pieces before reattaching them to the completed furniture.

Preparing to varnish

Each varnish manufacturer's formula is a little different from all the others, so it is important to read the product label very carefully before starting work. The following guidelines are general and should be disregarded if they differ from the manufacturer's instructions.

Of all the furniture finishes in general use, varnish is the most difficult to brush. Don't let that discourage you. Although it takes a certain knack and a little practice, the technique can be easily mastered by anyone who is willing to give a little time and attention to practicing. As with all furniture-refinishing techniques, it is highly advisable to make a trial run on a piece of scrap wood that's the same as or similar to the wood from which your piece is made.

Dust

Even a slight sprinkling of dust results in bumps, which ruin the usual smoothness of a varnished finish. Varnish picks up dust faster than any other finish; if you want the best results, rather elaborate precautions must be taken to ensure an environment that is as dust-free as possible.

To allow all the dust in the air to settle, begin your preparations a day ahead or at least 3 to 4 hours before you varnish. Start by dusting the work area. Close all windows and any heat or air-conditioning outlets. Vacuum the room thoroughly. Use the various attachments for your vacuum cleaner to get into corners and crevices, then go over the room with a tack rag to pick up as much residual dust as possible.

When the work area has been thoroughly dusted, go over the piece you intend to finish with the narrowest attachment for your vacuum. Then dust the entire surface of the piece with a clean tack rag.

To stir up as little dust as possible, move about slowly and deliberately as you work. Be sure to wear dust-free clothes. This may seem like a lot of trouble to go to, but it is well worth it. Dust is the greatest enemy of a smooth varnished finish.

Atmospheric conditions

Varnish only on a dry day in a warm room. Do not attempt to work in damp weather or on wood that is anything but bone dry. Be sure that both the varnish and the air temperature are at least 70° F. If you must work in a room that is colder than the recommended temperature, be sure to place the unopened can of varnish in a pan of warm water for as long as necessary to warm it up to a temperature well above 70° F.

Light

Place a lamp with a bare bulb to the side of the piece, opposite where you will be working. Work against a white wall or next to a window so you can spot imperfections such as lap marks, bubbles, and uneven coverage.

Mixing

Before removing the lid, hold the can of varnish in your hand and rotate it gently back and forth to mix the product. Never shake the can—this produces bubbles. Open the can and stir the varnish gently, taking care to prevent the formation of bubbles. Pour a small amount of varnish from the can into your working container, and loosely recap the can to prevent evaporation. (Although a varnished surface takes quite a while to dry completely, solvent evaporates in an open container, making the varnish thick and difficult to work with.)

If you find that the varnish is becoming a little difficult to brush, add a small amount of a thinner recommended by the manufacturer. If no thinner is recommended, play it safe and don't thin the varnish.

Equipment

Before you start, gather all the tools and equipment you will need. As well as drop cloths and tack cloths, you will need the following.

Containers

To avoid dust contamination and to control the amount of varnish on the brush, it is best to work with a specially prepared container. A shallow can is best, but a clean coffee can will do. Punch two holes opposite each other near the top of the can, and twist a length of wire coat hanger through the holes and bend the ends

back to secure. This serves as a strike wire—gently tap out excess varnish against it. Don't drag the bristles across the wire or the side of the can; this causes bubbling.

Brushes

Start with a brand-new, soft, natural-bristle brush. (Traces of solvent may remain in a brush that has been used before, and these could cloud the varnish.) It is a good idea to select one brush that is intended for use with varnish. The bristles hold more varnish than do those of a standard brush, and the finish goes on more smoothly. Varnish brushes are available at many paint-supply stores.

Stroke the brush across your hand a few times to remove any loose bristles. Then, with an empty brush, rapidly pretend to paint a clean wood surface for a couple of minutes to dislodge any bristles that are loose.

When you have made all other preparations and are ready to start, dip the brush into the varnish to a depth of one third to one half of the bristle length. Work the brush back and forth over a piece of clean paper. This distributes varnish evenly through the bristles so that you will get an even coat when you begin working on wood.

Applying varnish

Varnishing is slow work. If it isn't done slowly, the results will be poor. Work on a horizontal surface whenever possible. To do this, turn the piece from side to side as you work, allowing the side that has been varnished to dry before you turn it. Remove doors and drawers and work on them separately. Fluid varnish

levels itself after it has been brushed on, but it can only do so on a level surface. If you have to work on a vertical plane, varnish small areas at a time, brushing alternately down and up to catch runs.

When varnishing a chair or other tricky item, turn the piece upside down and do the legs first, using a narrow brush. Then turn the piece right side up and do the rest in the following order: back, front, arms, and seat. When brushing turned parts, such as chair and table legs, brush around the turnings but keep your strokes straight on the unturned areas. If varnish accumulates in carved areas, use a dry brush to pick up the excess.

The sealer coat

Every successful varnishing job consists of at least two coats: The first coat is often the sealer coat, which consists of the finishing product thinned considerably with solvent. Sealer coats are generally recommended over water-based stains, though they are not needed over wiping stains. Check the label to see if sealer coats are suggested with the product you are using and, if so, what thinner you should use. A typical sealer consists of 1 part turpentine to 4 parts varnish. Like every subsequent coat, allow the sealer to dry thoroughly, sand it lightly to remove any imperfections, and wipe carefully with a tack rag. To save yourself the trouble of dusting and vacuuming, it is a good idea to do any sanding away from the prepared work area.

Brushing technique

A coat of varnish should be laid down rather than brushed on like paint. Dip the brush to a depth of one third to one half of the bristle length and lift it straight up. If necessary, tap out excess on the strike wire.

Begin laying down the varnish on the point farthest from you and work in toward you. Apply the varnish to the piece thinly and evenly. Use long, smooth strokes—as few as possible. Brush either with or against the wood grain on the first pass. Don't attempt to brush out the varnish at this point. Overlap the strokes very slightly. Don't trail the brush off at the end of a stroke; lift straight up and dip it in the varnish again. Dip the brush as necessary while you work, to keep the varnish flowing.

When a small area of the surface has been coated—a section of about 6 to 10 inches square—quickly go back to the beginning point, and with the brush still partially loaded with varnish, stroke lightly at right angles to your first application, cross-stroking with just the tips of the bristles. This works the varnish well into the grain and smoothes out the finish. Look for uneven patches, runs, and bubbles and even them out. Finish off by brushing lightly with an almost dry brush, still working at right angles to the first coat. Hold the brush almost vertical as you do this. This final light brushing is called tipping off. It is important that you not attempt to varnish a large area before tipping off; if too big an area is covered, the varnish may start drying.

Pick up any stray bristles using a brush tip wet with varnish. Take special care when working near the side or varnish may run over the edge.

When the varnish has been laid down and tipped off, leave it alone to level itself and dry. Never attempt to touch up the surface with additional brushing or by adding more varnish.

If you spot an area where the varnish is leveling imperfectly, leave it. You can brush it more evenly when you apply the next coat.

Don't be disturbed by any dust specks you may see on the surface after the varnish has been applied. They can be taken out by sanding when the finish has dried. If the dust particles are especially big and unsightly, lift them off with an artist's brush. If you do this, be careful not to disturb the surface and be sure to do it before the varnish has begun to level off; otherwise, you will leave tiny craters in the finish.

Drying time

A first coat of varnish takes at least 24 hours to dry. Avoid touching a finish coat until it is completely dry. When you have finished for the day, leave the work area, close the door, and stay away. If the weather is rainy or humid, drying a first coat may take 48 hours or longer. Dry subsequent coats for at least two days. For best results, let the final coat dry for three days or longer before being sanded or otherwise smoothed.

Let the piece stand for the recommended time or until it seems hard. Test by pressing with your thumbnail in an inconspicuous place. If the surface is hard, test it further by making a thumbprint. Wipe the spot with a clean cloth and check to see if the mark remains. If there's even a trace of a print, leave the piece to harden further. Never apply an additional coat of varnish until the previous coat is completely dry.

Sanding between coats

After each coat of varnish dries, rub the surface lightly using 320- to 400-grit abrasive paper or 3/0 or 4/0 steel wool. If using abrasive paper, wrap it around a padded sanding block to prevent damage to the surface. Purists prefer wet sanding using

soapy water as a lubricant. Although this method reduces the possibility of damage, if you work carefully, it really isn't necessary.

Always sand between coats of finish. This knocks off dust bumps and other small imperfections and roughens the surface so the next coat adheres well.

Work with the grain, rubbing lightly and evenly. Be careful not to cut through the finish. Take special care when you work on trim or near the edges to prevent your abrasive from cutting through to the wood. Avoid cross-grain sanding when you work on places where different parts of the piece come together.

Continue to sand the surface until all the sheen is removed, then wipe thoroughly with a tack rag to remove varnish granules. Stroke the surface with your fingers to test smoothness.

Number of coats

Apply a minimum of two coats of varnish: a sealer coat plus at least one finish coat. When using flat or satin finishes, two coats is generally sufficient. With glossier varnishes, the finish improves with additional coats. Apply as many coats as needed to get the look that you want. For a very deep glossy finish, you may need as many as six or seven coats.

When the final coat is dry, polish surface with steel wool. Use 4/0 for a soft sheen and 6/0 for a glossier look.

Hand-rubbing

Sometimes a newly varnished surface has a brightly glistening look that is too shiny to be truly attractive. If you want your piece to have a warm, deep gloss that isn't shiny, hand-rub it. Even satin varnishes will be improved by hand-rubbing.

Traditionally, hand-rubbing was done with pumice and oil, sometimes followed by rottenstone and oil. Both pumice and rottenstone can be found

in most hardware stores, but automotive rubbing compound is a good modern substitute.

If you prefer the traditional method, sprinkle the piece with a very light machine oil. Spread it around with a felt pad until the surface is evenly covered.

Shake on a sprinkling of the finest grade of pumice available. (A salt shaker makes a good applicator.) Rub surface lightly with the pad. Be gentle; you are working with an abrasive.

When you have done a small area, wipe the surface with a clean rag and examine the piece. If you like the effect, continue to rub the entire piece. If the surface is still too shiny, apply more oil and pumice and rub

until you achieve the desired look.

When the entire surface has been rubbed, clean off the oil and pumice with a clean cloth. Wipe on a coat or two of fine paste wax and buff.

Produce a finer, richer effect by substituting rottenstone for the pumice or by using automotive rubbing compound. After the final light sanding or polishing with steel wool, rub on the compound with a clean rag or a piece of felt (a blackboard eraser works well). Work with the grain. Keep rubbing until the varnish takes on a glassy smoothness. This will take time; keep rubbing. When you have a finish that pleases you, wipe with a cloth, apply a good furniture paste wax, and buff to final perfection.

Empty wine bottles can be turned into convenient applicators by cutting a thin groove in the cork. Then fill the bottle with the finish of your choice, replace the cork stopper, and shake small amounts on the surface of the piece you are working on. Keep only working amounts in these bottles. All finishes should be stored in tightly sealed containers.

SHELLAC

Shellac produces one of the most beautiful of all furniture finishes. For centuries it has been the traditional finish for fine furniture, particularly mahogany. Shellac is the first choice among the transparent finishes for objects that don't get heavy wear. It is also the basis for the elegant classic method of furniture finishing known as French polish (see opposite page).

Shellac is a completely natural product; no synthetic version has been developed. The preparation consists simply of the secretions of the tiny lac insect suspended in alcohol. Found only in India, the lac insect feeds on the sap of trees and leaves resinous deposits, which harden on the branches. The collected resin is dissolved in denatured alcohol.

Despite its beauty and comparative ease of application, shellac has some serious disadvantages. It is because of these disadvantages that the popularity of shellac has been diffused by durable modern synthetics. Shellac stains easily, softens in spilled alcohol and other chemicals, blooms (turns white) when exposed to water, and has poor heat resistance. It follows that shellac should not be used on tabletops, cabinets, or any place where hot pans, drinking glasses, or decanters might be placed. However, there is no finer finish for chairs, benches, desks, sofas, racks, picture frames, and clocks.

Shellacked finishes are not durable and need touching up from time to time. Since the finish dissolves easily in alcohol, this is quite easy to do, by using the process known as reamalgamation (see page 40).

Buying shellac

The proportion of resin to alcohol is known as the cut. Cuts of shellac are measured in terms of the number of pounds of shellac flakes that have been added to one gallon of denatured alcohol. Thus, a 4-pound cut consists of 4 pounds of shellac flakes in 1 gallon of alcohol. It isn't very important which cut you buy, since you can change the concentration by simply adding alcohol to heavier shellacs. A 1-pound cut is the concentration that works best on furniture. A 1-pound cut can be made from a 4-pound shellac (the most common available) by adding 3 parts denatured alcohol to 1 part shellac.

Always buy plenty of denatured alcohol when you buy shellac. Working with shellac that is too thick is a common mistake. Time may be saved, but the results will be poor.

The thinner the shellac, the more coats are required. One-pound shellac is quite thin, so count on laying down 3 to 5 coats to produce a good finish. One-pound shellac brushes on easily, dries quickly, and can be recoated in only a few hours, so you can shellac your piece of furniture in a day or two, despite the number of coats needed.

Don't store shellac. It undergoes chemical changes and deteriorates quickly. Therefore, buy only as much as you need for a given project. Since shellac loses drying properties even in an unopened container, use it before the expiration date on the can. Once the container has been opened, the finish will spoil in about 6 months; after this, the product simply will not dry properly.

Types of shellac

White and orange shellac are the most common available types.

White. White shellac, made with bleached shellac gum, is a milky mixture that dries without color and is particularly suitable for blond finishes. It also looks attractive over light stains and on light-colored woods.

Orange. Orange shellac is transparent with a reddish tone, which slightly tints the wood. It should be used on dark woods such as walnut and mahogany. It can also be used over metal leaf to simulate gold.

Orange shellac resists water a little better than does white and lasts somewhat longer in the can. Unfortunately, the two types of shellac cannot usually be mixed, and intermediate shades are unavailable.

The work space

Work in an environment that has been made reasonably dust-free, and vacuum your piece and dust it with a tack rag. Work in a warm, dry atmosphere—humidity causes drying shellac to bloom with white patches. Set up good lighting to spot surface defects: Position a bare bulb opposite from where you will be working and close to the surface of the project.

Application techniques

If you have not already sealed the entire surface of the piece, do so with a coat of shellac thinned to about half the consistency of 1-pound shellac. Stir the shellac gently as you thin it. Don't shake the can—shaking causes bubbles to form.

Pour out a small amount of shellac into a clean, shallow container. Use a new, good-quality, soft-bristled brush, and dip it in shellac from one third to one half the bristle length. Flood the brush and gently press out the excess against the side of the can. Apply the finish to horizontal surfaces, turning the piece as necessary. Lay the finish down in slow, smooth-flowing strokes. Work slowly enough to avoid making bubbles but fast enough so that the edges don't begin to dry before the next stroke overlaps. Brushing over drying shellac causes buildups and makes for an unsightly patchy look. Overlap only slightly to minimize buildup. A little patchiness is not too critical—it will come out if you sand between coats. As a new coat is laid on, it softens the previous coat and bonds with it. No matter how many coats you apply, they will all bond into a single coat. As with lacquer, shellac finishes are built up out of applying successive coats. Nevertheless, for the smoothest possible effect, each coat of shellac usually is sanded.

The first coat of shellac dries quite rough. Let it cure, then sand it with 400-grit abrasive paper. Working with the grain and in one direction only. Use open-grained paper be-cause granular shellac clogs up the paper very quickly. Avoid back-and-forth sanding—it could cut through the finish and, because shellac is heat sensitive, too much friction could cause the film to soften and blur. If you do cut through, don't worry. The next coat will fill in and bond with the sanded coat. Test the surface with your fingertips. If it's smooth, wipe with a clean cloth and apply the next coat.

Smooth every coat in the same way as the first, but realize that each coat will require a little less sanding. Continue to put on coat after coat until the desired effect is achieved. This may be as few as three coats or as many as six or even more. You will know that you are close to the final coat when you see the shine that you want begin to come up.

After your final coat has dried, go over the surface with very fine steel wool. Dust the piece, wipe it with a tack rag and a clean cloth, and leave it to cure for a day or two before applying paste wax.

For the very finest high-gloss shellac finish, allow the surface to cure for three days or more and hand-rub the piece with pumice and rottenstone. Rub on paste wax and buff at least 24 hours after the hand-rubbing has been completed. If you use a power buffer, remember that too much friction will soften and distort the surface, so keep the buffer moving.

French polish

Anyone working with antiques should know how to apply a French polish, the classic shellac finish. This deep and luxurious translucent finish is obtained by applying coat after coat of shellac and linseed oil and rubbing each coat into the furniture surface. French polish is the finish seen on great antiques of the classic styles—Sheraton and Chippendale, for example—but this finish is by no means restricted to collectors' items. Many fine contemporary pieces are French polished in order to bring out the full beauty of the wood.

Only custom carpenters and amateurs now use this finishing technique which, although not particularly difficult, does require a lot of time—and elbow grease.

Not only is the finish beautiful, it is tough and, if damaged, can be easily repaired. The process brings out the depth and iridescence of the grain, and the final result is a lustrous patina with a high sheen that continues to deepen with repolishing.

Preparation

Preparations for applying a French polish are the same as preparations for other clear finishes: Work in a warm, dry, dust-free room. Carefully sand and stain the wood with a water-based stain (the process will lift other types of stain). Fill any open-pored wood (see page 52).

The applicator

French polish is applied with a cloth pad dipped in linseed oil to prevent it from sticking.

Any piece of soft, clean, lintless cloth can be used as an applicator. Pieces of gauze, cheesecloth, muslin, linen, and cotton will all work very well. A much-washed T-shirt is also suitable. Fold the cloth into a 6-inch square pad or wad an old nylon stocking into a ball. The pad should be as wrinkle-free as possible.

Above: Really good wood should be stained and given a lustrous clear finish. French polishing, the method that produces the finest effect with shellac, brings a deep, rich glow to an armoire door.
Opposite: The recommended type of finish is the one that best suits the intended use of a piece of furniture. On a dining table, for instance, a water- and alcohol-resistant polyurethane is a good choice.

Application techniques for French polish

Pour some boiled linseed oil into a shallow dish and some 1-pound-cut shellac into another. Dip the pad into the oil and go over the piece, wiping the oil lightly onto the surface. Then dip the pad lightly into the shellac and even more lightly into the oil. Squeeze out any excess into a waste receptacle and pull any wrinkles out of the applicator pad.

Rub the shellac-and-oil mixture onto the surface, going with the grain at first to fill it but switching quickly to a rubbing motion of overlapping circles. Carefully blend the strokes—this circular rubbing motion is the basis of the polishing technique. Begin the motion before the pad comes into contact with the wood. The rubbing must be continuous—the pad will stick and lift the finish if it is ever allowed to rest on the wood. Lift the pad from the surface with a sweeping motion so that it never rests on the piece for even an instant.

Repeat the process: Dip first into shellac, then oil, squeeze the pad, and rub on the mixture, keeping the pad continuously moving in overlapping circular strokes until the entire surface has been covered several times. Continue to rub on the finish for as long as it transfers to the surface, working the polish into the wood. This constitutes a coat.

Let the finish dry completely before putting on another coat. Never sand between coats of French polish. The mellow sheen increases as more coats are rubbed on. There is no limit to the number of coats that can be applied, but three coats are considered the minimum.

As you gain skill in French polishing, you can graduate from 1-pound-cut shellac to heavier cuts, such as 4- and even 5-pound cuts. This speeds up the process because the coats are denser. Early coats should contain more shellac than oil, but use less shellac and more oil with each coat. As the finish deepens, discard the pad and use the heel of your palm lubricated with oil to polish the surface of the piece.

If there are pad marks or excess oil on the surface after the final coat has been applied, remove them with a clean rag dipped in denatured alcohol and wrung out until it is damp-dry. Be careful—the alcohol causes the shellac to reamalgamate slightly (see Reamalgamation on page 40) so use just a hint of alcohol. Otherwise, the finish may soften noticeably.

As with other shellac finishes, French polish can be mellowed and softened by hand-rubbing with pumice and rottenstone. Complete the finish with careful paste waxing.

LACQUER

Lacquer is extensively used in the furniture industry and by custom woodworkers because it can be sprayed on and it dries quickly. But these same qualities make it one of the more difficult finishes for the average do-it-yourselfer.

Spray lacquers require spraying equipment, and the speed at which brushing lacquers dry makes it essential to work fast. Lacquer is available in aerosol cans, but these are useful only for small projects.

A lacquer finish is an attractive option for some home projects, however, and the skills needed can be acquired with a little practice. The rewards of mastering lacquering are certainly worth the trouble; a successful lacquering job results in a brilliant, jewel-like surface. In addition to the mirror-smooth luster, lacquer is one of the more protective finishes. A lacquered surface looks very much as though it has been shellacked, but unlike shellac the surface is resistant to heat, water, and alcohol. In addition, lacquer also darkens wood less than almost any other finish.

For projects that call for a less brilliant surface, the bright shine can be toned to a warm sheen by sanding with steel wool or hand-rubbing. Because of the brightness and clarity of tone, lacquered surfaces are more appropriate on smaller pieces such as decorative wooden items, picture frames, mirror frames, lamp stands, jewelry boxes, and small chests of drawers. Larger pieces usually appear to better effect when finished with coatings with less shine.

Safety first

Lacquer contains acetone, which is highly volatile, and it usually also contains nitrocellulose, an ingredient found in gunpowder. Nothing that emits flames should be anywhere near your work space. This includes such sometimes overlooked sources of flame as stove and furnace pilot lights, automatic water heaters, and faulty electrical appliances. Take strict precautions to ensure that no one smoking a cigarette comes near lacquer. The flammable nature is enhanced when the finish is sprayed; brushing is safer. As a further precaution, always wear a painter's mask when you are brushing with lacquer. If using a spray gun, always wear a respirator. Lacquer is toxic and should not be inhaled.

Applicators

Lacquer can be applied with a pad, brush, spray can, or a spray gun. In most cases the end result will be about the same. The choice of applicator has more to do with safety, the equipment you have available, legal considerations, and how much care you want to take. In a few instances, however, the type of wood to be finished is a factor. Some exotic hardwoods—rosewood, for instance—contain resins that will become muddy if lacquer is dragged around on them with a brush.

Spray guns

Most home refinishers find it impractical to use a spray gun. The first reason is a legal one: All cities and most towns have codes restricting the use of spray equipment because of the flammable, potentially explosive nature of the material. Expensive, heavily insured spray booths may be set up in industrial locations, and you may be able to pay for the use of one in a place such as a body shop. But it is illegal to spray lacquer with a spray gun in your home if you live in a city.

Using a gun and air compressor makes for fast, efficient work, but even if you own this equipment, are willing to buy it, and live where you can legally use it, you will also need to construct an enclosed spray booth since the sprayed lacquer gets into the air. An adequate spray booth incorporates exhaust fans, exit and entry filters, and explosionproof light fixtures. It is clearly not practical for most people to use a spray gun.

Aerosol spray cans

It is practical to use aerosol spray cans of lacquer at home, and these can be useful for small projects. Remember to take the same safety precautions when using an aerosol as when applying lacquer by any other method: Do not work anywhere near open flame and always wear a mask.

Aerosol sprays are fairly easy to use and don't leave brush marks, but they don't produce as fine and well directed a mist as an adjustable gun nozzle. However, even aerosol sprays are somewhat troublesome. They are difficult to use on horizontal surfaces and tend to cause runs when sprayed on vertical ones. There is also the problem of the sprayed mist hanging in the air and settling on surrounding surfaces.

Many people find that spraying is more trouble than it is worth; this is particularly true with lacquer.

Brushes

Brushing lacquer is the preferred method for the do-it-yourselfer. Brushing is much less dangerous and complicated than spraying. Although the technique takes a certain knack that should be practiced before starting work on a prized possession, the end result can be very satisfactory.

Preparation

Lacquering calls for much the same preparation as varnishing. Preparation of the wood surface, however, has to be even more exacting.

Water-based and non-grain-raising stains work best under lacquer; lacquer tends to dissolve oil-based stains. If your piece has been stained with an oil-based preparation, seal the surface with shellac thinned with denatured alcohol. Don't sand it, just brush lacquer over the dry shellac.

No matter what stain has been used, the first coat of lacquer should be a thin sealer coat. This doesn't necessarily mean that the preparation should be diluted; just spread small amounts over fairly large areas. A thin coat of shellac (shellac diluted with denatured alcohol in a proportion of about 4 parts alcohol to 1 part shellac) also makes an excellent sealer for lacquer. If you have used sanding sealer on the piece, a sealer coat won't be necessary. (Sanding sealers work particularly well with lacquer since the sealer is itself a type of lacquer.)

A coat of lacquer reveals every tiny surface defect, so give your piece a thorough critical examination. Look at it from various angles under a bright, unshaded light. Work on the surface with superfine abrasive papers and steel wool until it is as perfect as you can get it. Then vacuum the piece thoroughly and go over it with a fresh tack rag. Lacquer does not pick up as much dust from the air as varnish because it dries more quickly, but the work area should be as dust-free as possible. Vacuum the work area carefully and dust with a tack rag.

Application techniques

Although the fast drying time (usually 4 hours or less) makes lacquer somewhat difficult to work with, there are advantages: Dust doesn't have much time to settle, and it is possible to build up several coats of finish within a day. However, fast drying doesn't necessarily make lacquering a fast process. High-quality lacquer finishes call for exacting surface preparation and, if sprayed on, a meticulously followed schedule of application.

Brushing lacquer is much like brushing varnish, but lacquer dries much faster. Thin the lacquer according to the manufacturer's instructions until it flows easily. Use a wide brush to help spread the lacquer on quickly. Be sure to make a trial run on scrap material to get the feel of how the finish goes on and how quickly it dries. Dip the brush shallowly to soak the bristles. Don't rub or tap out an overloaded brush; squeeze out the excess by pressing the brush on the side of the can.

When you begin working on your piece, apply lacquer in bold, long strokes, keeping back-and-forth brushing to a minimum. You will notice that lacquer tends to dry more quickly at the edges of the brushed area, so it will be easier to get an even coat if you do only a small area at a time. Put lacquer on sparingly and quickly, without much brushing in. It will flow out by itself.

Drying time

Lacquer dries in only a few minutes, but sometimes manufacturers' recommended drying times are misleadingly short. For best results always allow at least 4 hours between coats.

Each coat of lacquer softens the previous one and bonds chemically, making sanding between coats unnecessary in most cases. Occasionally, a light sanding is needed to knock off dust bumps or to level out high spots. For the most brilliant finish, polish each coat with dry abrasive paper. Start with paper no coarser than 320 grit and work down to 500 or 600 grit for final polishing.

Number of coats

How many coats of lacquer should you apply? The answer is simple but nonspecific: Apply as many as necessary to get the effect you want. Lacquering is not simply a covering job. Poor lacquering reveals two surfaces: the surface of the coating and the surface of the wood. Fine lacquering is the result of building up and polishing down many coats to produce one gleaming surface.

Hand-rubbing

The brilliance of lacquered surfaces can be toned down and given qualities of warmth and depth by handrubbing with pumice and rottenstone. Use exactly the same method as is used when hand-rubbing varnish. (See page 64.)

OIL FINISHES

Finishing with oil is one of the oldest methods of enhancing the qualities of good wood. Classic hand-rubbed oil finishes are among the most subtly beautiful of all wood surfaces. Many people think they are the most attractive of all furniture finishes.

Best suited to close-grained woods, oil finishes give a warm, deep sheen that can't be duplicated by other finishing methods. Oil finishes always darken the wood they are applied to, so if you want to preserve the light tone of your piece of furniture, do not consider them.

An oil finish is fairly resistant to heat, water, and alcohol stains and, when properly applied, resists scratching. It is also the easiest of all finishes to apply, but note that easy does not necessarily mean quick.

There are several good reasons why oil finishes are no longer as widely used as they have been in the past. Although oil finishing is easy to do, the process takes a long time to complete. In a sense it is never complete since the piece has to be re-oiled once a year to keep up the finish. And wood finished with natural oils collects dust as no other finish does. Reserve natural oil finishes for antiques when your aim is period authenticity. For modern furniture, use the more convenient synthetics. These can be put on very quickly, they do not collect much dust, and they are much more resistant to stains and scratches than natural products.

Linseed oil

Boiled linseed oil is the basic traditional oil finish, though tung oil is sometimes used. Both products are derived from crushed seeds, and application methods for both oils are about the same. When buying natural finishing oil, look for boiled linseed oil. Raw linseed oil is available but it is not recommended—it does not contain driers, so the finishing process takes even longer.

Only water-based stains should be used under oil finishes because oils work by penetrating the wood whereas water-based stains leave the surface porous.

Mix 2 parts boiled linseed oil and 1 part turpentine. You can apply undiluted oil, but the thinner improves spreading and penetration. The mixture can be applied hot or cold; it goes on more readily when heated. Remember that turpentine is flammable, however. Heat the preparation in a can that is placed in water in a double boiler. It only takes a few minutes to warm it up.

Brush the mixture onto the wood surface and let it dry until it penetrates the wood and loses its gloss. This should take about 10 minutes. Wipe off the excess with a clean cloth. (A hard cloth, denim for example, is best.) Continue to polish the surface, and keep rubbing briskly until the surface glows.

Apply several coats of oil the first day. Then put on one coat a day for a week, one coat a week for a month, one coat a month for a year, then one coat a year for the life of the furniture.

Tung oil

There are several modern finishing products based on tung oil; these are generally two-stage applications. The first contains a stripping compound that removes the previous finish without damaging the underlying stain.

The second component is a mixture of tung oil and modern synthetic resins—a mixture that is easy to spread on with your bare hands. The warmth of your hands will help the oil to penetrate.

These systems are the easiest of all finishing methods to use, and it's hard to make mistakes as long as you follow the manufacturer's instructions to the letter. If you are finishing bare wood, the two-stage applications are available in kits with stain included.

Penetrating resins

These finishes are synthetic products rather than petroleum-based oils. Like the other oil finishes, they are easy to apply, but unlike them they are as quick as they are easy to use. They are the ideal finishes for the natural-wood look and are often applied to unstained surfaces, particularly softwoods such as pine. Most of them darken the wood and intensify the color, but almost colorless versions are available as are versions pigmented to match wood tones. The lightest of the pentrating resins is often sold in home-center stores labeled as Danish oil.

Penetrating resins sink into the wood fibers and, when they harden, strengthen as well as finish the wood surface. For this reason, the durability of softwoods finished with these resins is much improved.

Penetrating resins are never brushed or sprayed. They are wiped on with pads and smoothed and polished with a cloth. A typical finishing job takes about three days since each coat should dry for about 24 hours and three coats are usually needed. Each brand is applied slightly differently—be sure to read and follow the manufacturer's instructions.

WAX

Wax is better for furniture than polish is, and it protects wood better. Paste wax makes an excellent final finish for all the clear finishes, especially shellac.

Paste wax and beeswax

These waxes, melted and thinned with turpentine, can be used as a primary finish for hardwoods, but wax is usually applied over some other clear finish to protect it from grime and wear. Never use wax to finish bare softwoods if there is any likelihood that the wood will be finished with some other material in the future—wax enters and clogs pores, making it impossible to remove.

Lemon oil

Some experts do not like the qualities of a waxed surface and recommend the use of lemon-oil polish to clean and protect the finish. Lemon oil, a cedar oil colored yellow and scented with lemon, is used to moisturize wood that is losing natural oils and drying out. Use it sparingly. If you don't care about the lemony scent, a bottle of mineral oil from the drugstore works just as well and costs much less.

Application techniques

Be sure your piece is well dusted before applying paste wax. Put about 2 tablespoons of wax in the middle of a piece of tightly woven cloth and fold the cloth over the wax. Rub the surface of the piece with a circular motion until the entire finish is covered with a film of wax. Let it dry. Now rub the surface with a clean, soft cloth such as flannel. After rubbing

thoroughly, switch to a harder cloth and rub some more.

Too little polish or wax leaves your furniture unprotected, but too much makes your piece a dust trap. Moderation is the secret to good waxing and polishing. Two coats of wax is the minimum; three make a piece look even better. Test the surface with your finger. If you can't see a fingerprint, you haven't used enough wax or rubbed it enough.

All wax and natural-oil finishes occasionally need renewal, although an excess will build up in time. Read and follow the manufacturer's instructions for removing excess.

Wax can be used as a finish although it requires maintenance. It is more commonly applied as a final finish to protect and add gleam to any clear finish.

SPECIAL EFFECTS

Standard finishes are not suitable for every piece of furniture, and they do not look appropriate in all situations. If a piece is badly damaged, for example, a novelty paint finish or trompe l'oeil might be a good way to rejuvenate it. Stenciling and decoupage add character to dull pieces. The type of finish should also suit the setting. Refined, highly polished finishes look best in a formal setting and on elegant furniture.

Many special effects are available to the home finisher, though some, such as trompe l'oeil and certain forms of gilding, call for plenty of confidence and some practice. Others, such as marbling, graining, and fuming, are within the capabilities of anyone who wants to take a little time and care to add distinction to otherwise ordinary furniture.

Skillful decoration can give new life to a badly worn piece or one with wood that is not worth refinishing.

FUN FURNITURE

For many people there is no finish more satisfying than the gleam of well-finished and polished wood. Although it is certainly true that the fascinating rings, whorls, and patterns of a piece of fine wood should not be obscured, there are pieces of furniture that will look better if the finish is opaque.

You may own a piece that you particularly enjoy because you inherited it, or because it fulfills a useful function, or merely because you like the way it looks. Maybe the wood isn't that special or maybe it is so badly worn and stained that it would require too much effort to restore the finish. If either of these drawbacks apply to a piece that you have stashed away but can't bear to part with, this chapter is for you.

In recent years, there has been a very definite swing away from the white-wall look of the past two decades. "Less is a bore" has become the credo for many architects and interior designers. Color, pattern, and texture are all very much in evidence. Pinks and grays, popular in the fifties, are enjoying a revival and are being used on both the inside and outside of homes. In keeping with this interest, the following pages are intended to inspire you to think about finishing possibilities that are more decorative.

In addition to the vast array of colors available in paint, there are several techniques that add interest

Above: *The use of a strong color can turn a roomful of unfinished or unmatched furniture into a custom-designed statement.*
Opposite: *Flat surfaces are easier for the do-it-yourselfer to work on when experimenting with special finishes. Here, a simple console table is painted to coordinate with the hand-painted silk wallcovering that lines the bedroom.*

Opposite: A simple bookcase is given character with a specialty finish. This look can be achieved by spraying unfinished wood with automotive paint.
Above: Turning a lackluster buffet into a decorative focal point requires a great deal of artistic skill. But it can be done—with paint.

and texture to the surface. Striping, spattering, sponging, and combing are some of the ways to add texture to a painted surface. These techniques are not new; marbling, stenciling, and other *faux* finishes were all popular in Victorian times. Although these finishes require a certain amount of skill, the necessary tools can usually be found around any home— brushes, sponges, and combs.

Many of the finishes that follow are an ideal way to make something special out of a piece of ready-made unfinished furniture. Many stores across the country sell reasonably

priced cubes, bookcases, and storage pieces made out of particleboard or pine. These pieces are often well designed but rarely suitable for merely staining and sealing. By using one of the *faux* finishes, you can make the particleboard look like marble or tortoiseshell. You can add stenciled or handpainted designs. You can even bead the edges with strips of bamboo. The intent is to create a piece of fun, decorative furniture that adds to the decor of your room.

ANTIQUING

Commonly known as glazing, antiquing is an easy way to simulate the mellow, aged look that comes from many years of wear. Never use antiquing techniques on a true antique; you will destroy its value.

This type of finish is a two-step process. First you apply an enamel-based coat of one color, then a coat of glazing material of another color. The appearance of a complex patina is achieved by wiping the glaze before it dries.

Glazing kits containing all the necessary materials are available in most paint stores, but the look can easily be achieved by using an enamel of your choice, a glaze (highlighter) that is a home-mixed or commercial preparation, and one of a wide variety of wipers (sponges, paper towels, cloth pads, for example).

Suitable colors

Color choices for the base coat are unlimited. Paint dealers can blend almost any shade of enamel for the base coat.

Glazes can also be any color if you make your own, but most commercial applications are in the earth colors—raw umber is standard, though white and gold are available. The glaze can be lighter or darker than the base coat, although darker shades are usually preferred.

Commercial glazing kits give you an idea of what the popular color combinations are. But frosting with a highlighting glaze can produce original and attractive finishes with little difficulty, so use your imagination!

If you want to glaze your piece in a shade not commercially available, make your own glazing liquid by mixing 1 part oil-based enamel in the color of your choice with 3 parts clear varnish. Dilute the mixture with an equal volume of turpentine.

Preparation

The wood doesn't have to be stripped bare, but do sand off any gloss from the previous finish. New, unfinished pieces should also be sanded to give some tooth to enhance bonding. Particularly coarse-grained wood should be filled and sealed (see pages 52 and 53).

Prime the piece with an undercoat if recommended by the manufacturer of the enamel you are using.

Base coat

If you make up your own glazing kit, be sure that the base-coat enamel and the enamel in the glaze are compatible by checking to see that both can be thinned with the same solvent.

Lay down the enamel finish following the usual methods for varnishing and enameling. Always keep in mind that you are not painting the surface; you are finishing it with long, smooth brushstrokes. Cross-brush and tip off to even and blend out brush marks.

Allow about 24 hours drying time after the first coat, then sand with 320-grit abrasive paper. Apply a second coat (two coats should be sufficient) and, when dry, sand it with 400-grit paper.

Glazing

Glazes can be applied over stains as well as enamels, but if you choose to do this, be sure to seal the stain with a wash coat of clear shellac.

Apply a thin, even coat of glaze with a soft brush. Wipe it lightly as it dries with a plastic sponge or paper towel. The longer the glaze is allowed to dry before wiping, the more pronounced the antiquing effect will be. As you wipe, keep in mind the natural effects of wear and tear. Wipe away more glaze in the places that would be handled or otherwise worn if the piece were actually an antique. Sharp edges always get worn and should be noticeably highlighted with the wiping.

Protect glazed surfaces and give them an attractive shine by applying a final coat of varnish.

Dark color in areas that normally accumulate dust adds years to the appearance of a newly refinished chair.

DISTRESSING

Distressing a piece of furniture means adding subtle signs that simulate normal effects of age and wear.

D istressing is a natural complement to the antiquing technique discussed opposite. Careless handling is no disadvantage when taking this approach. In fact, it's what is called for. Distressing consists of nothing other than treating furniture with calculated roughness; knock it around and strike it to simulate an aged and worn appearance.

Mar new, unfinished pieces before they are finished—hitting a new finish with a hammer or a burlap bag containing chains goes beyond creating the suggestion of age and use. Use any hard object to mar the wood: tools, rocks, keys, whatever. To simulate the worm holes that often appear on antiques, pierce the wood with a nail or other pointed object.

Successful distressing calls for imagination and restraint. Damage only the parts of the furniture that would be naturally worn with age. For example, round off hard edges with abrasive paper, wood rasps, or files; pit and mar tabletops to suggest that they have been well used.

It is very easy to overdo distressing. Be judicious. The piece should look comfortably used, not vandalized.

Be discriminating about the type of furniture you distress. Some pieces should look unblemished. Surfaces beneath a French polish, multiple coats of hand-rubbed varnish, and jewel-like lacquer should all be as perfect as possible, although small imperfections, such as the maker's tool marks, enhance the appearance and even the value of older pieces and of true antiques.

MARBLING

Not surprisingly, marbling is a method of making wood look like marble. A ground color is applied, and then a marble texture is worked over it in another color. The most successful approach is usually to use this technique to create a fantasy effect rather than an exact imitation of marble—trying to reproduce the subtleties of marble is a slow, difficult technique.

The ground coat should be a cream, semigloss enamel. When this coat is dry, sand lightly to remove any brush marks or other slight imperfections in the finish.

Apply a coat of white glazing liquid and, while the glaze is still wet, dab on patches of beige or buff enamel. Shade the edges of these patches with green or bluish black artists' pigment thinned to the desired color tone with turpentine. Use an artists' brush to apply the color, and shade and soften the veining with a soft, clean cloth.

Allow the piece to dry for 24 hours or more, then finish with a semigloss polyurethane varnish.

Reproducing the subtle graining of marble is a process that requires a background glaze and artistic sweeps of a contrasting color.

STENCILING

Stenciling is easy to do, inexpensive, versatile, and attractive. You merely paint through a paper, cardboard, metal, or acetate template (stencil). Use stenciling to perk up plain, utilitarian pieces such as footstools, chests, footlockers, and children's play furniture.

Oiled stencil paper, acetate sheets, and stencil knives are available from art-supply stores, but improvised templates made of shirt cardboards cut out with a sharp knife will suffice. Make sure that the material used for the template is tight grained enough to prevent seepage.

Draw a design on the stencil paper by working freehand or using a T-square, compass, triangle, and curve. It's a good idea to keep your design simple until you are familiar with the technique. As you gain confidence, your designs will be limited only by your imagination.

When the design is drawn, you are ready to cut out the stencil. A drawing board is an ideal cutting surface, but any flat surface will do. Be sure to protect the working surface from cut marks by cutting over some protective material. A piece of plate glass or safety glass is ideal, but thick cardboard will also serve as a buffer.

Cut toward you, keeping the knife blade at a 90-degree angle to the surface. Doing so prevents undercutting, which results in smearing when the paint is applied.

When the template is completed, position it on the piece of furniture with tape. Use a tape that will not mar the finish. Cover the area around the template with newspaper. If using spray paint, be sure that all edges of the template are masked with tape;

sprayed finishes tend to find their way under loose edges.

Whatever paint or enamel is used, make sure it is thick enough—a finish that is too thin seeps under the template. Spray or brush the design evenly, avoiding paint buildup in any one place. Stencil brushes—which have a thick clump of stiff bristles cut square on the end—work well, but spray cans of paint or enamel produce good results. If you prefer to brush in the design, use enamel for large areas but artists' tube paints mixed to a workable consistency with turpentine for more intricate parts of the design.

The appearance of most stenciled pieces is improved by sealer coat of varnish over the entire piece. This will also protect the design from chipping. If you spray the design, use a spray varnish of a formulation similar to that of the stencil paint.

To coordinate furniture in a bedroom, trace designs from the wallcovering, the rug, or a bedspread, and use these shapes to paint a stenciled design on a chest of drawers or a bedside table.

GILDING

A special piece of carving, such as this doctor's emblem, becomes even more distinguished when gilded.

Gilt is often used in furniture finishing as trim and to provide light touches in trompe l'oeil. It also serves to highlight a special piece of carving.

The original gilding process, which is called water gilding, is a difficult technique that requires expensive materials. Because it involves applying genuine gold leaf to a colored ground of gilding clay it is beyond both the means and the skills of the average do-it-yourselfer. Fortunately, there are several alternatives to genuine gold leaf that don't require getting a loan from the bank.

Many crafts stores sell books of relatively inexpensive imitation gold leaf called schlagmetal. Imitation gold leaf, which is much easier to handle than real gold leaf, is sold in 5½-inch-square sheets, 25 sheets to a book. Packs of 10 books are available.

Even when using oil gilding, the contemporary technique that is considerably less demanding than the traditional water gilding, the application of metal leaf is tricky and time-consuming. (Leaf gilding is a process of applying an adhesive, placing very thin sheets of metal on it, smoothing down the metal, and burnishing. Oil gilding uses an oil-based medium as an adhesive.) Many do-it-yourselfers prefer to use the uncomplicated modern imitation gilding methods that employ either metallic powder or liquid gold-leaf paint instead of leaf. A still simpler method is wax gilding with gold-tinted paste.

Applying gold leaf

Whether you are gilding a frame, a jewelry box, or a decorative carving on a piece of furniture, begin by sealing the wood with thinned orange shellac and sanding lightly when dry with 150-grit abrasive paper. Next, brush on two coats of burnt sienna acrylic paint. Use the type that comes in a tube, and thin it with an equal amount of acrylic medium. (Both the paint and the medium are available at art-supply stores.) Allow the paint to dry overnight, then sand. Apply two more coats of undiluted orange shellac, sanding between coats.

The adhesive that holds the leaf in place is called size, an oil-based varnish made especially for gilding. For best results, use slow-drying size, which takes about 12 hours to reach the proper tack and retains tack for another 12 hours. Following the manufacturer's application instructions, apply as thin a layer of size as possible. The size will not feel tacky to the touch when it is ready for the leaf to be applied, but it will hold the leaf. Be careful to avoid fingerprints.

Use a dry, very clean brush to slide a sheet of leaf onto a piece of cardboard. A special brush known as a gilding tip is available for the purpose, but a soft 1½-inch paintbrush will do. Use scissors to cut the leaf, then transfer it to the sized surface on a piece of cardboard slightly larger than the piece of leaf. Take care to place it correctly. If you try to move it once it has been placed on the size, it will tear. If it's a little crooked, overlap the next piece to fill the gap. The overlap can be easily dusted away with a dry paintbrush at a later stage. Leaf isn't elastic, so don't try to stretch it into place. Cover high sections first, then fill in lower areas. When the section you are working on is covered, rub the leaf with a cotton ball to make sure the entire area contacts the size. Rub in the direction of the overlaps, not against them. The hairline edges will become part of the final antiquing.

It is unlikely that anyone's first attempt at gilding will be satisfactory. Gilt wrinkles easily, and size tends to smear. Early attempts should be considered test runs. Sand off the faulty gilding, reprime wood as necessary, depending on how much shellac and acrylic paint have come off with the leaf, and try again. It will take some practice to learn the technique.

After gilding, seal the surface with the same thinned shellac used to seal the wood. Then coat with undiluted orange shellac to give a mellow tone to the gold. When the shellac is completely dry, brush on a coat of brownish-black antiquing toner. Wipe off high spots with a paper towel or a clean cloth; leave more toner in the low spots. This gives a streaky highlighting to the gilt. To create additional depth in the antiqued finish, stipple the surface with tiny spots of black and brown by dabbing a paint-dipped toothbrush close to the surface. A light flecking of paint is all that is needed.

Working with the grain, use fine abrasive paper or steel wool to "age" the surface by exposing traces of the red ground color. As a final step, preserve the finish by brushing on a coat of the clear acrylic medium.

Metallic powder

Use these fake-gold products light-heartedly rather than as serious imitations of real gold. Do not use a metallic powder on a piece with real gold—the genuine metal will show up the powdery thinness of the imitation. Follow manufacturer's instructions for mixing and application.

Wax gilt

Wax gilt is an inexpensive gold paste that is rubbed on with the fingers to freshen existing gilt finishes. It is often used over liquid gold-leaf paint, which is itself frequently used to touch up damaged gold leaf. Working through a cloth, use your fingers to rub wax gilt over dry paint. Buff the dry surface to bring up the luster.

Gilding highlights the striations in the posts of a late-19th-century bed. Gilt can also be used to dramatize picture frames and mirror surrounds.

BLEACHING

The reason to use bleach when finishing a piece of furniture is to make the overall color of the piece brighter and lighter, thus producing the blond look that is currently fashionable.

Some woods bleach more readily than others. Maple, walnut, oak, mahogany, and birch are fairly easy to bleach; pine and redwood are rather difficult. In general, hardwoods bleach more easily than softwoods. Many softwoods and some maples often have a faded, dingy appearance after stripping. Bleaching brightens and lightens the color before finishing.

Using bleach safely

All bleaches are highly caustic and will burn almost anything they come in contact with. Take great care when working with them and follow these pointers.

☐ If you splash yourself with bleach, rinse the affected area immediately with water.

☐ If you get bleach in your eyes, flush eyes thoroughly with warm water and go to a doctor immediately.

☐ Rubber gloves are a must when working with commercial furniture bleach.

☐ A rubber apron and safety glasses are recommended.

☐ Wear a dust mask when sanding a bleached surface; you certainly don't want to inhale particles of bleach.

☐ Never sand before the bleach has been thoroughly neutralized; bleach crystals are highly caustic and toxic.

Types of bleach

There are three types of bleach that are generally used in furniture refinishing. These are chlorinated household bleach, oxalic acid, and commercial wood bleach.

Chlorinated household bleach

Household bleaches like Clorox brand are the mildest and safest wood bleaches. These are principally used to remove spots rather than to bleach entire surfaces. Household bleach removes ink, dye, and water stains. It works well on maple and walnut but is not effective on dark-toned woods.

Dilute chlorinated bleaches with 1 part water to 1 part bleach. If used full strength, they may produce an undesirable yellowish or greenish coloration. Household bleaches can be neutralized with white vinegar used at full strength or with ordinary soap and water.

Oxalic acid

If laundry bleach doesn't give you the result you're looking for, bleach with oxalic acid. Oxalic acid is a medium-strength bleach that works best on light, open-grained woods and is useful for taking out stains that may result from the stripping process.

You can find oxalic-acid crystals at drugstores and hardware stores. They are very effective on oak, particularly for removing water stains. Oxalic acid tends to leave a slight pinkish tone on the surface.

The usual proportions for mixing oxalic acid solution are 3 ounces of acid crystals to a quart of hot water, but be sure to follow the instruction given on the product label. Wet the wood surface before brushing on the hot solution of oxalic acid. Allow each application about 20 minutes to work before neutralizing it.

Commercial wood bleach

This kind of bleach is the strongest available for wood. It is applied in two separate solutions: the first usually consists of sodium silicate or lye and the second, of concentrated hydrogen peroxide. Both solutions are dangerous, so use with caution. Two-solution bleaches are best applied when you intend to bleach an entire piece; they are difficult to control for spot bleaching. They are capable of bleaching most woods white if used repeatedly, so don't overdo. Follow the manufacturer's directions exactly.

Application techniques

Before you bleach be sure the surface of the piece is extremely clean. If you suspect that any wax remains from the stripping chemical, wash the piece thoroughly with turpentine, wipe it with a clean rag, and allow to dry completely.

Apply the bleach with a nylon brush (natural bristles deteriorate in bleach), stroking with the grain. Brush the bleach on evenly, making sure it is evenly absorbed. Proceed slowly; take care not to flood the surface; this can cause irregular absorption. Use cotton swabs for spot bleaching. Let the bleach work until the wood is the desired shade. This may take 15 minutes or it may take up to 24 hours, depending on the type of bleach used.

Neutralize the bleach with vinegar or a mixture of borax and warm water. The solution should consist of one cup of borax to one quart of warm water or white vinegar at full strength. Brush on the solution, taking care not to miss any areas.

When the bleach has worked and has been completely neutralized, rinse the wood with clear water, dry thoroughly with a clean cloth, and allow the piece to stand for 24 hours. All bleaches raise the grain somewhat, as does the final wash down. Therefore, sanding after bleaching is essential. (Bleach crystals are highly caustic; never sand before the bleach has been completely neutralized.)

Pale, blond woods have become fashionable in modern interiors. To remove the red coloring from this mahogany chair, the wood is being bleached.

FUMING

Fumed oak was a popular finish in the early part of this century. Nowadays most do-it-yourselfers choose fuming because they want to match the finish of antique oak furniture, though walnut, chestnut, and mahogany can also be fumed.

Suitable woods

Fuming is done by exposing wood to ammonia, which reacts with the tannic acid in the wood to produce darkened areas that highlight the grain. The color can also be changed from an obviously new pale yellow or white to an antique-looking rich dark gray, black, or greenish brown. The success of the fuming process depends on the natural amounts of tannic acid that exist in the wood being treated. Oak and chestnut both contain large amounts of tannic acid and will change color readily. Woods with less tannic acid—mahogany and elm, for example—will only change color

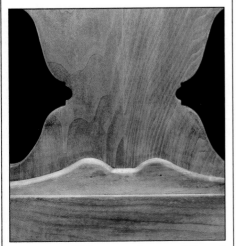

Walnut acquires a subtle and uncharacteristic look when exposed to ammonia fumes.

slightly unless the wood is first primed with acid. The final color is determined by the length of time that the piece is exposed to the ammonia gas as well as the strength of the solution. Experiment to discover the range of color and tone that is made possible by the fuming process.

Fuming techniques

Some exposure to the ammonia is inevitable, and since it will irritate the eyes and nose and cause choking and coughing, fuming must be done outdoors or in a very well-ventilated room. Wear a painter's mask over your mouth and nose, and flush your eyes with warm water if necessary.

You will need an airtight container. For very small projects, a plastic box with a snap-on lid will do. For larger pieces, make a container of black plastic sheeting sealed with duct tape. (The sheeting must be opaque because sunlight will make the color uneven.) Build a tent-like structure to accommodate the piece by knocking together a wooden framework to support the plastic. Never use metal supports, and be sure to remove all hardware from the piece—ammonia causes wood to burn black at any point where it comes in contact with metal. Be sure that any seams are tightly sealed with tape, including the edge where the sheeting reaches the floor. In some cases it may be necessary to disassemble the piece to fit it into the container.

You will also need several saucers or shallow containers and aromatic spirits of ammonia, which are available at any drugstore. (These are often used to revive people who have fainted.) Ordinary household ammonia can be used, but it will work much more slowly.

Set the furniture to be fumed in the sealed container, and place several saucers containing spirits of ammonia around it. Space the saucers so that the fumes will be evenly distributed.

Glance into the container from time to time to check the coloring of

the wood. Fumed wood goes through a range of colors, from honey yellow to a medium brown. Take the piece out of the container when it is approaching the desired shade. Don't leave it in until it has reached the color you want—ammonia continues to darken the wood even after you take the piece out of the container. It usually takes about 24 hours for the wood to darken to the maximum.

Finishing fumed furniture

Once you are satisfied that the piece has been sufficiently fumed, remove it from the container and place outdoors. It will smell awful and, if it has been exposed to ammonia for some time, it may take several days before the smell evaporates. Sometimes there will be a blackish-purple deposit clinging to the surface of the fumed wood. This is easy to remove by rubbing the affected spots with wire wool that has been soaked in methylated spirits.

Fumed oak may be varnished, shellacked, or lacquered, but the traditional finish is wax. Commercial paste wax, which is usually tan, harmonizes well with the color of the wood. If you wish, darken the wax by adding a little burnt-umber artists' pigment.

Black wax on fumed oak creates a dramatic finish that was popular in the 1920s. The finish looks especially attractive on pieces from that period, and it is also flattering to contemporary pieces. To produce black wax, liquefy commercial paste wax by placing the container in a pan of hot water over heat. The water should not boil. Add lampblack or other black pigment to the liquid wax, let it harden, and apply it to the piece of furniture. The dark wax accumulates in the pores of the wood, throwing them into sharp relief, but it is too thin to noticeably affect the color of the other parts of the wood.

DECOUPAGE

This striking decorative technique dates back to the seventeenth century, when small art prints were applied to furniture and preserved with lacquer.

Decoupage may be done on bare or finished wood surfaces, and almost any two-dimensional decoration can be applied. Use a large illustration or map to cover the entire top of a card table, for example. Or place small keepsakes such as calling cards, invitations, postcards, postage stamps, photographs, and prints onto any flat surface to create a lighthearted decorative effect.

If you have chosen an illustration with printing on the back, seal the back with a coat of white glue thinned with water, and allow it to dry. This prevents the printing from showing through.

Before applying the decoration, the wood surface must be completely prepared for the application of a clear finish and as clean as you can get it. If you are working on bare wood, that means the piece must be thoroughly sanded, filled (if necessary), sanded again, and sealed with wood sealer or a thinned coat of the intended clear finish. (Remember, sealer coats must also be lightly sanded before applying finish coats.)

If the surface has been stained or enameled, prepare it just as if you were applying a clear sealer coat. Touch up as necessary and remove all minor imperfections. Remember that the finish and the undercoat must be compatible, or capable of being thinned with the same solvent.

Depending on the desired effect, pictures may be carefully cut out with scissors or torn out, leaving a ragged edge. If the decoration is torn out, lightly sand the ragged edges on the back so they lie flat. Determine the location of the decoration and apply some white glue thinned with water

to the piece and to the back of the decoration. Lay it carefully in place and smooth it with your fingers, working out creases and air bubbles. Lay a sheet of waxed paper over the decoration and roll out excess glue (a rolling pin works well). Wipe the excess away with a damp rag. Brush the front of the decoration with the glue solution, and allow the glue to dry.

You are now ready to finish the piece. You can use any clear finish—shellac, lacquer, varnish, liquid plastic, or even antiquing glaze—as long as you are sure that it is compatible with the sealer, stain, or undercoat already on the furniture. Cover the wood and the decoration with finish, allow to dry, sand lightly, and wipe clean. Sand between multiple coats of finish. The actual number of coats necessary depends on the finish used. Apply as many as are needed to make the decoration appear as if it were in the wood surface, not on it.

The art of decoupage comes to the aid of people who lack painting skills but wish to decorate a piece of furniture. This screen is a wonder of Victorian cutouts.

GRAINING

Even an ordinary piece of plywood can take on special charm when it is finished with a painted wood grain.

Graining is usually applied to liven up the surface of otherwise ordinary wood such as undistinguished pine, birch, plywood, or composition wood. Graining involves applying a finish that imitates the grain of a desirable surface.

Successful graining takes practice, but before you start learning the technique, study samples of the wood you intend to imitate. Notice that the natural patterns in wood are never uniform, and keep in mind the fact that too much repetition produces an unnatural effect. Good graining isn't a mechanical skill. Improvise; be spontaneous when you work.

A considerable variety of tools is available for graining; all produce different effects. However, for most graining projects, the essential tool is a steel or rubber graining comb.

Effective graining depends on a good ground coat that duplicates the color of the lightest part of the wood that is to be imitated. A flat latex enamel makes an ideal ground. Graining stain, available premixed, is applied over this.

Since there are as many graining effects as there are different woods, instructions are given only for two of the most frequently applied finishes: oak and brush graining. The latter produces a generic type of grain.

Oak-graining technique

To apply an imitation oak finish, apply a base coat of flat cream-colored enamel to a well-sanded surface. When this is dry, rub on oak-graining stain, following the manufacturer's instructions. Allow the stain to set until the surface looks flat and dull (usually 10 to 30 minutes).

Simulate oak grain with a rubber graining comb. Hold the comb at a 45-degree angle and keep the teeth as parallel with the surface as possible without touching the surface with your hand.

Apply a coat of polyurethane when graining is completely dry.

Brush-graining technique

This technique depends on imagination; brush graining makes no attempt to imitate real wood. Therefore, both ground coat and graining color may be of any color. Many effects are possible, so use your own taste and decorative color schemes to decide on a combination. It is a good idea to keep the ground color pale. Other than that, colors are a matter of preference—raspberry over sky blue, bottle green over light green, blue green over pink. Various paints and enamels can be used, but a reliable combination consists of a glazing liquid over a flat enamel, both oil based.

When the base coat is dry, apply the liquid glaze and begin graining while it is still wet. Drag the tips of a coarse-bristled brush or a whisk broom through the wet glaze with a rippling, wobbling motion. Try to create the general appearance of wood grain, but don't make it either too uniform or too irregular. Most of the lines should be flowing and curving, but remember that trees usually contain knots and jagged heartwood, so simulate these features occasionally.

If you wish, vary basic brush graining by wiping the graining lightly with a soft, clean brush to produce a flecked, blurred effect. Professionals use a special brush called a flogger to achieve this look, but any soft-bristled brush will do.

Apply a coat of polyurethane when the graining is completely dry.

Painted grain can be done either realistically, to fool the eye, or with some poetic license, to turn an undistinguished cabinet into a very special piece.

TROMPE L'OEIL

*A pigsty in your living room?
It might appear so, but looks
are deceiving. Both pigs and chicken
wire are painted on this cabinet.*

When a piece of furniture is just not interesting enough or the wood is not good enough to be refinished, consider painting a witty, amusing, or decorative "scene."

Trompe l'oeil (literally "deceiving the eye") requires a great deal of artistic skill but, when done well, creates a dramatic effect. The idea is to make the two-dimensional scene or image appear three dimensional and real, tricking the eye of the beholder—if only for a moment—into believing that the image is something other than what it really is.

Almost any piece of furniture is a candidate for trompe l'oeil but the scene you paint should be suitable for the size and shape. It is also essential that the painted objects be colored realistically and scaled life-size otherwise the effect will be lost. Select a theme that will emphasize the appropriateness of the disguise. For example, paint "tiles" on the doors of a bathroom vanity that match the real ones on the wall.

If your painting skills do not extend beyond spreading on white paint with a roller, this finishing technique is not for you. But if you can draw well enough to realistically copy an object or decoration, trompe l'oeil is a medium with which you can have fun. Choose things that are simple to reproduce—a shelf of books or a trellis screen, for example. Realize that you don't have to paint the entire piece freehand. You can incorporate decoupage techniques (see page 89) and stenciled borders and patterns (see page 83).

As with any kind of finish, you must first prepare the surface. Follow the instructions given in the section on Enamel that follows for both types of products and techniques.

ENAMEL

Enamel is often recommended as a finish for a piece of furniture made out of low-quality wood. It is also used to cover pieces made from different, contrasting types of wood. But enamels have also been used on good furniture for centuries.

Not only does enamel protect and preserve, it also produces quality decorative finishes. Fine Pennsylvania Dutch furniture was usually painted, as were some great Sheraton and Louis XV and XVI pieces.

Enamel is pigmented varnish; therefore, it is applied in the same way as a clear varnish and has the same durability and stain and mar resistance.

Types

Today enamels are available in a wide range of synthetic formulations. Alkyds, acrylics (also called latex), and polyurethanes are the types of colored enamels usually found on dealers' shelves. All work well on furniture and have the same qualities as their varnish counterparts. Before deciding on a particular type, look over Synthetic Varnishes, page 61).

Alkyd-based enamels are oil-based. They are washable, durable, and suitable for use indoors or out, and they provide a strong, shiny, dirt-resistant finish. Polyurethane enamels are very tough and resistant to heat and marring. Latex enamels (acrylics) are durable and easy to work with. It is also easy to clean up afterward because they are water-based. However, latex enamels are not available in high-gloss finishes.

To strip these built-ins would have been a gargantuan job. However, restoring the badly scarred wood with a coat of gleaming enamel merely required careful sanding to provide a smooth painting surface.

Finishes

Enamels are available in gloss, semi-gloss, and flat finishes. All produce good results, but flat enamel is usually unappealing on furniture. If you want a shiny but not supershiny finish, it is sometimes better to rub down a high-gloss surface than to use semi-gloss enamel.

Colors

The color choice in enamel is now unlimited since your dealer can blend any shade you want. Paint dealers stock an enormous number of tiny color chips that serve as samples of standard blends, and many dealers also custom blend to match a fabric or other material. Bring along a sample of what you want to match when you shop for enamel.

Preparation

Whether enameling a finished or an unfinished piece of furniture, you must first prepare the surface.

Prepare the piece by removing as much of the hardware as possible. Make the room and the piece as dust-free as you can by using a vacuum cleaner and a tack rag. When you begin enameling, try not to stir up dust when you move about. Enamel doesn't show dust as easily as does varnish, but the result will be smoother if you take precautions. Work in a room that is at least 70° F. A dry atmosphere is best. If you work in wet or humid weather, close the windows and allow extra drying time between coats.

On finished surfaces

It isn't always necessary to strip a piece down to bare wood before applying enamel, even if there is enamel on it already. It is necessary to smooth the surface with abrasive paper, however. You must remove all gloss. Commercial deglossing liquids are available for this purpose, and if you use one sanding is not necessary if the surface is smooth.

Cracked, chipped, or sticky finishes should be taken off with varnish remover. If the old surface is only dirty, wash it with detergent and water and degrease it with mineral spirits or the enamel manufacturer's recommended solvent.

When applying enamel to a stained surface, it is a good idea to spot test a small area to see if the stain bleeds through. If it does, remove the enamel and seal the entire surface.

On unfinished surfaces

If new wood has knots or other flaws that may ooze sap, clean them with solvent and apply sealer to the affected areas. Putting a light sealer coat of white shellac or other sealer over the entire piece is a good idea if the unfinished wood is coarse-grained. Coarse-grained woods should also be filled (see page 52) before being sealed.

Primer coat

Priming or undercoating may not be necessary, but if it is recommended by the manufacturer (and it usually is for bare wood), apply it.

A thinned coat of the finish enamel may work well as a primer, but for best results, use a commercial undercoat. Undercoats are sold in basic white but can be tinted by adding a small amount of the surface enamel. Apply the undercoat by using the same brushing technique used for enamel (see Application Techniques).

Give an undercoat at least as much time to dry as the manufacturer recommends; allow more time in damp weather. Sand the dry undercoat with abrasive paper of about 180 grit.

Application techniques

Stir the enamel thoroughly but gently to prevent bubbling. Apply the finish to a horizontal surface whenever possible by turning the piece as necessary. Enamel settles and levels out by itself if laid on a flat surface.

Brush it on using long, smooth strokes. Apply the coating to the surface without brushing in, working in one direction. When you near the edge of the piece, carry the strokes out past the edge, taking care to prevent dripping. When a small area has been done, go back over it without redipping the brush, brushing at right angles to the first strokes and working with the tip of the brush to tip off (to even and smooth out) the enamel. The first coat of enamel goes on more easily if it is slightly thinned. However, you should not thin any of the subsequent coats.

Allow the enamel to dry as directed (usually for 24 hours), then sand with an open-grained, fine-grit abrasive paper. Be sure to dust the surface thoroughly after sanding. Repeat the sanding procedure with a very fine abrasive paper after subsequent coats.

Two coats of enamel are often enough, but a third coat may be applied for extra gloss. Sand the final coat only if the surface is too shiny. Dull it slightly by rubbing with wet abrasive paper and a mixture of water and mineral oil. You can take it down to a satin sheen by hand-rubbing (see page 64). Paste waxing is recommended to protect the surface.

INDEX

A
Abrasive papers, 48
Alligatoring, 40
Animal glues, 12
Antiquing, 80

B
Beeswax, 73
Black wax, 88
Bleaching, 47, 86
  for stain removal, 41, 42, 43
Blooming, 40
Broken edges or corners,
  32–33, 41
Broken runners, 31
Burning, as stripping method, 44.
  Burns, 42
Butt joint, 16

C
Casters, repairing, 28
Chairs
  repairing, 22–23, 31, 35
  sanding techniques, 51
  types of, 22
Chemical strippers, 44
Chipped edges, 32–33, 41
Clamping, 12, 13
Clamps, 6, 14, *15*
Cleaning wood, 10
  before gluing, 12
  before stripping, 46
  stripping vs., 10
Clear finishes, 60–72
  French polish, 67–68
  lacquer, 70–71
  oil, 72
  restoring, 43
  shellac, 66–68
  varnish, 61–65
  wax, 73
Cracked finishes, 40–41

D
Dado joint, 16
Danish oil, 72
Decoration, 75, 79
  decoupage, 75, 89
  gilding, 84–85
  sanding techniques, 51
  stenciling, 75, 79, 83
  trompe l'oeil, 92
Decoupage, 75, 89
Dents, removing, 41
Distressing, 81
Doors, repairing, 26
Dovetail joint, 16
  disassembling, 21
Doweled joint, *16,* 17
  in chair, 22
  disassembling, 21
  nails for pinning, 11
  in table, 24
Doweling jig, 17
Drawers, repairing, 11, 29

E
Edges or corners, repairing,
  32–33, 41
Enamel finishes, 93–94
  holes or scars in, 43
  identifying, 10
  marbling techniques, 82
Epoxy, 12

F
Fasteners, 11
Faux finishes, 79
Fillers. *See* Wood fillers
Finishes; Finishing
  See also specific kinds
  antiquing, 80
  bleaching before, 86
  choosing, 8–9, 59, 60, 75
  clear, 60–72
  color considerations, 59
  compatibility with stain, 55
  distressing, 81
  enamel, 93–94
  faux, 79
  French polish, 67–68
  fuming before, 88
  gilding, 84–85
  graining, 90
  identifying, 10, 40
  lacquer, 70–71
  marbling, 82
  novelty paint, 76–79
  oil, 72
  overcoating, 43
  reamalgamating, 40
  removing, 44–47
  restoring, 39–43
  shellac, 66–68
  special effects, 75–94
  staining before 55–57
  stenciling, 83
  trompe l'oeil, 92
  unfinished furniture, 6
  varnish, 61–65
  wax, 73
Fir, 8, 9
  sealing, 53
Fish glues, 12
Food stains, removing, 43
French polish, 67–68
Fuming, 75, 88

G
Gesso, 30
Gilding, 75, 84–85
Glazing (antiquing), 80
Glue injector, 12, 21
Glues, 12
  applying, 12–13, 21
Gouges, 42–43
Grain, simulating on patches, 43
Graining, 75, 90
Grave, defined, 34

H
Hand-rubbing
  lacquer, 71
  varnish, 64–65
Hardwoods, 809
  See also Woods
  sanding problem, 51
Hinges, repositioning, 26

I
Identifying the finish, 10, 40
Identifying wood, 8–9
Ink stains, 41
Interior defects, repairing, 34

J
Jelled wiping stains, 57
Joints, repairing, 12, 21, 22, 24

L
Lacquer, 60, 70–71
  cleaning cautions, 10
  identifying, 10
  padding, for overcoating, 43
  reamalgamating, 40
  sealing under, 53
Laminating runners, 31
Lap joint, 16
Latex enamels (acrylics), 93
Latex wood fillers, 42
Legs, repairing, 35
Lemon oil, 73
Linseed oil, 72
Lye, 44

M
Marbling, 75, 79, 82
Metallic powder, 85
Mineral oil, 73
Mortise-and-tenon joints, 16
  repairing, 22, 24

N
Non-grain-raising (NGR)
  stains, 57
Novelty finishes, 75, 76–79

O
Oak, 809
  filling, 52
  fuming, 88
  graining, 90
Oil-based stains, 55–56
Oil finishes, 60, 72
  cleaning vs. stripping, 10
Oxalic acid bleach, 86

P
Padding lacquer, for overcoating, 43
Paint finishes
  See also Enamel finishes
  identifying, 10
  marbling techniques, 82
  novelty, 75, 76–79
  stenciling, 83
Paint remover, 44
Paste fillers, 52
Paste wax, 73
Patching
  broken edges or corners,
  32–33, 41
  interior defects, 34
  simulating grain, 43
  veneer, 36–37
Patina
  preserving, 44, 48, 49
  simulating, with antiquing, 80
Penetrating oil stains, 56
Penetrating resins, 72

(no letter)
Pigmented oil stains, 55–56
Pinned joints, disassembling, 21
Plastic finishes, 61
Polyurethane enamels, 93
Polyurethane finishes, 61
Pumice, for hand-rubbing
  varnish,64–65

R
Rabbet joint, 16
Reaamalgamation, 10, 40
Refinishing, 39–43
  choosing a finish, 8–9, 60, 75
  choosing furniture for, 6
  restoring vs., 6, 39
  sanding before, 48–51
  sealing before, 53
  staining before, 55–57
  wood fillers, 42, 52
Repair, 19–37
  See also specific furniture items
  broken or chipped edges,
  32–33, 41
  casters, 28
  checking alignment, 13
  checklist of defects, 20
  choosing furniture for, 6
  disassembly, 12, 21 , 26, 29
  fasteners for, 11
  gluing, 12–13, 21
  hinge repositioning, 26
  interior defects, 34
  joints, 12, 21, 22, 24
  replacing missing parts, 30
  sequence of, 20
  surface defects, 39–43
  veneer, 36–37
Resorcinol, 12
Restoring finishes, 39–43
  refinishing vs., 6, 39
Rocking chairs, repairing, 31
Rottenstone, 64–65
Router, for shaping patches, 33
Rung joints, repairing, 22
Rungs, repairing, 22, 23
Runners, repairing, 31

S
Safety
  with bleaching, 41, 86
  in chemical stripping, 45
  with lacquer, 70
  when sanding, 50, 51
Sanders, 49–50
Sanding, 48–51
  before gluing, 12
  as stripping method, 44
Sanding blocks, 49
Sanding sealers, 51, 53
Scratches or gouges, 42–43
Screwed joints, on table, 24
Sealer coat, 53
  with shellac, 67
  with stain, 57
  with varnish, 63
Shellac, 60, 66–68
  See also Stick shellac
  cleaning cautions, 10
  French polish, 67–68
  over gesso, 30
  identifying, 10, 44
  reamalgamating, 10, 40
  removing buried paint with, 47
  sealing, 53, 67

Softwoods, 8–9
See also Woods
joining with screws, 11
penetrating resin finish for, 72
sanding problem, 51
sealing, 53, 57
Spindles
replacing, 23
sanding techniques, 51
Spot bleaching, 42, 43, 86
Spot refinishing, 41
Spray guns, 57, 70
Stain (blemish) removal, 40, 41, 43, 49
Stains; Staining, 55–57
color and, 55, 59
removing, 47
replacing, 41
sanding before, 51, 57
sealing with, 53, 57
Steaming dents, 41
Steel wool, 49
Stenciling, 75, 79, 83
Stick shellac or lacquer, 42–43
for broken edges or corners, 32
for concealing nails, 11

Stick wax, 42
Stripping, 44–47
for alligatoring, 40–41
cleaning vs., 10
for dents, 41
restoring finish vs., 6, 39
Surface defects, repairing, 39–43

T
Tables
polyurethane finish for, 61
repairing, 24, 25, 32–33, 35
Tools, 6
See also specific jobs
clamps, 14, *15*
doweling jig, 18
lathe, 6, 23
power sanders, 49–50
Tourniquets, 13, 14
Trompe l'oeil, 75, 92
gilding with, 84
Tung oil, 72

U
Uneven legs, 35

Unfinished furniture, 6
enameling, 94
faux finish for, 79

V
Varnish, 60, 61–65
cleaning vs. stripping, 10
identifying, 10
sealing under, 53, 63
Varnish remover, 44
Veneer
buying, 36
identifying, 44
repairing, 12, 36–37
sanding techniques, 51
Vinyl coatings, 61

W
Warped furniture, 25, 26, 29
Washing. See Cleaning wood
Water-based stains, 56–57
Water spots, 40, 41, 42
Wax, 60, 73
black, 88
in chemical strippers, 44

cleaning vs. stripping, 10
water protection with, 41
Wax gilt, 85
White glue, 12
in gesso, 30
White rings, 41, 41, 49
Wiping stains, 55–56
jelled, 57
Wobbly tables, 24
Wood bleach, 86
Wood cleaners, 10
Wood dough, 32, 42
Wood fillers, 52
epoxy as, 12
for patching, 32
for scratches or gouges, 42
Wood putty, 32, 42
Woods
choosing stains for, 55–57
finish choices and, 8–9, 59, 60, 75
identifying, 8–9
joinery, 16–17
sanding problems and, 51
Wood seal, 53

U.S. Measure and Metric Measure Conversion Chart

		Formulas for Exact Measures			Rounded Measures for Quick Reference		
	Symbol	When you know:	Multiply by	To find:			
Mass (Weight)	oz	ounces	28.35	grams	1 oz		= 30 g
	lb	pounds	0.45	kilograms	4 oz		= 115 g
	g	grams	0.035	ounces	8 oz		= 225 g
	kg	kilograms	2.2	pounds	16 oz	= 1 lb	= 450 g
					32 oz	= 2 lb	= 900 g
					36 oz	= 2 1/4 lb	= 1000g (a kg)
Volume	tsp	teaspoons	5.0	milliliters	1/4 tsp	= 1/24 oz	= 1 ml
	tbsp	tablespoons	15.0	milliliters	1/2 tsp	= 1/12 oz	= 2 ml
	fl oz	fluid ounces	29.57	milliliters	1 tsp	= 1/6 oz	= 5 ml
	c	cups	0.24	liters	1 tbsp	= 1/2 oz	= 15 ml
	pt	pints	0.47	liters	1 c	= 8 oz	= 250 ml
	qt	quarts	0.95	liters	2 c (1 pt)	= 16 oz	= 500 ml
	gal	gallons	3.785	liters	4 c (1 qt)	= 32 oz	= 1 l
	ml	milliliters	0.034	fluid ounces	4 qt (1 gal)	= 128 oz	= 3 3/4 l
Length	in.	inches	2.54	centimeters	3/8 in.		= 1 cm
	ft	feet	30.48	centimeters	1 in.		= 2.5 cm
	yd	yards	0.9144	meters	2 in.		= 5 cm
	mi	miles	1.609	kilometers	2-1/2 in.		= 6.5 cm
	km	kilometers	0.621	miles	12 in. (1 ft)		= 30 cm
	m	meters	1.094	yards	1 yd		= 90 cm
	cm	centimeters	0.39	inches	100 ft		= 30 m
					1 mi		= 1.6 km
Temperature	°F	Fahrenheit	5/9 (after subtracting 32)	Celsius	32°F		= 0°C
					68°F		= 20°C
	°C	Celsius	9/5 (then add 32)	Fahrenheit	212°F		= 100°C
Area	in.²	square inches	6.452	square centimeters	1 in.²		= 6.5 cm²
	ft²	square feet	929.0	square centimeters	1 ft²		= 930 cm²
	yd²	square yards	8361.0	square centimeters	1 yd²		= 8360 cm²
	a	acres	0.4047	hectares	1 a		= 4050 m²